STONE COLD
IN A WARM BED

One Couple's Battle with Pornography

by
Kathryn Wilson
with Paul Wilson

Horizon Books
Camp Hill, Pennsylvania

Horizon Books
3825 Hartzdale Drive, Camp Hill, PA 17011
www.cpi-horizon.com

ISBN: 0-88965-150-7

98 99 00 01 02   5 4 3 2 1

To my husband, Paul, who cared enough.

With special thanks to my dear friend,
Debra Alexander, who was encouragement per-
sonified and to Denny Morse, who modeled Jesus
to Paul and gave him back his hope.

CONTENTS

FOREWORD

I T HAS BEEN SAID that traumatic events shatter the spirit and kill its hope for wholeness. Pornography creates this kind of trauma, inflicting damage upon every life it touches. Men, women and children are all hurt by it; no one is immune to its toxic effects.

Pornography creates a misguided representation of what the most important relationships in life are supposed to be like. For some, these unhealthy expressions of sexuality are a means of escape; for others they are a form of self-medication. However, the end result is the same for all—pornography prevents its users from living in a state of truth, integrity and peace.

Pornography separates and isolates by destroying relationships. It puts distance between us and others, between us and God. It attacks the human spirit through shame, sexual addictions and profound confusion as to what "normal" sexuality really is. In the end, it destroys our capacity for intimacy.

Sexual addiction in a marriage can shatter all trust and faith. It reduces normal love and commitment to mere words and created illusions. The resulting damage can be so extensive as to force one partner to leave the relationship, in some cases removing the children as well. This is not always the case, however. Some relationships can and do survive this traumatic injury, but the emotional repair process is long, painful and challenging.

Despite the trauma caused by an addiction to pornography, there is hope. Those couples who share a spiritual foundation and a genuine commitment to each other, who honestly and openly seek healing, will meet with success. They may even find that the emotional repair process can rebuild their relationship in ways they never imagined possible. *Stone Cold in a Warm Bed* portrays such a renewal, taking the reader on the authors' journey back to hope and faith, wholeness and renewed commitment.

This book is an excellent resource for Christian couples coexisting in the shadows of a sexual addiction. It is also a unique guide for couples who until now have never considered seeking a spiritual foundation for their healing. Kathryn M. Wilson, with her husband Paul, has written a deeply moving personal account of meeting the challenge of this struggle in her own marriage. More importantly she understands what one must do and not do to heal.

This simple yet beautifully written guide serves to comfort, inspire and uplift. Based on Scripture, it is a straightforward approach that educates the reader with compassion and wisdom. Professional counselors and clergy will also benefit from the insights this book offers to those struggling to overcome this complex form of addiction.

Stone Cold in a Warm Bed is an eloquent reminder to partners of those sexually addicted that they are not alone. The author's style reflects her faith and resiliency as she shares exactly what readers need to hear and understand. Couples wrestling with sexual addiction and the impact of pornography undoubtedly will be blessed in an extraordinary way through the Wilsons' story.

Debra Whiting Alexander,
Ph.D., LMFT, CTS

INTRODUCTION

T HIS BOOK IS NOT a clinical discourse on the dynamics of addiction. It is not a technical manual filled with graphs and the latest statistics on sexual addiction. This is one couples' story. It is my story. It is a book about how sexual addiction has impacted one couple. It is a book about pain and forgiveness. It is a book about loss of hope and hope regained.

When you wrestle with addiction in your home, you do not have the energy for long, technical dissertations. At least, I didn't. You sometimes barely have the energy to pick up a book and read the words on the page. You find it hard to concentrate for long periods of time. You want to know that somebody understands. You want to know that somebody else has been there, that you're not the only one. You want to know that this pain will end and that there is hope.

This book is one couple's experience with sexual addiction. One couple's experience with anger, bitterness, rage, love and forgiveness. Being a Christian couple did not mean we could not be touched by sexual sin. We were touched. We were deluged. We were inundated. That we are still together is a blessing from God. We could not have made our way through this, still holding each other's hand without the Lord. Not a chance.

We have chosen to rebuild what was torn down. Rebuilding is not for cowards. It takes courage and strong determination. Disclosure and forgiveness are painful and difficult. I found the real test is standing side by side with the addicted partner and rebuilding destroyed trust brick by brick. All the while knowing that, because of this addiction, this person whom you love deeply and who loves you could be pulling the bricks off the wall when your back is turned.

I have been faced with the true test of forgiveness, the "seventy times seven" test. I have survived and so can you. Quitting would be easier. Quitting is always easier. At least for the small space in time when the pressure is off, and you are flooded with relief and freedom. However, joy does not come from quitting. Joy comes from perseverance, knowing that you can keep faith with yourself and your God, and knowing that you can do all things through Christ who strengthens you.

Recently, I heard someone say that all writing should lead people back to Christ or it is just psychobabble. This book will fail in its purpose if it does not lead you ultimately back to the Redeemer. Paul and I can write this book only because of Him. And because of Him, we wish you joy in your journey of healing and rebuilding!

Publisher's Note: While the Wilsons worked closely together on this book, the chapters were written by Kathryn with Paul's perspective and response presented in a different type face at the end of each section.

In the
First Light of Dawn

*Finding Out for Sure
What You've Known All Along*

Waking up early, unable to sleep. All of the emotions and feelings of the night before washing over me. So awake! Feeling cold in a warm bed. So cold, nothing can touch it. Stone cold! All lightness and joy gone, exploded away. Only the debris left over from the bomb. Hearing his breathing in the emptiness of the room. Wanting it to stop. Feeling guilty for even thinking such a thing.

I DON'T KNOW WHEN I first had a suspicion that my husband had a problem with sexual addiction. I know it was fairly early in our relationship. At first, it was just a feeling, an uneasiness, a distance. On some level, I "felt" something was wrong, that there was a problem. I had misgivings about our marriage. An entry in my journal from the days before our wedding reads, "Is Paul real? Does he mean this or does he just feel a response to my caring? Will he always do this push/pull thing? Can he give me what I need?"

But I was also confident I could deal with whatever problem might come up between us. Over the years, I had handled many difficult things in my life fairly well. My father died in 1978. It was an excruciating shock. Absolutely no warning. Though I was devastated, I quickly recovered and went on. Then there was the court battle with the natural father of a foster child I had reared from five months to six years. When the father won, our whole family felt a tearing loss. Not long afterward in August 1982, after a routine checkup, my first husband received a diagnosis of leukemia. He died a year later. I spent the next twelve months going from shock to hope to despair. Three major losses in four years. But I survived it all and felt I came through pretty well. I was strong. If problems arose in our marriage, I was convinced I could do whatever was needed to set it right.

All the incidents that aroused my suspicions could be explained. Most of the explanations my husband gave me were believable. I accepted them because I wanted to. However, there were lots of signs. Too many. They all seem so obvious from my present perspective.

When I met my husband, he had pornographic movies and magazines in his possession. He tried to draw me into his use of pornography with explanations that this was normal, and this was what he liked. I felt I should at least see what he was watching and decided to watch with him. I was uneasy, but didn't want to be a spoilsport. Soon, I became uncomfortable with this use of material for sexual stimulation and asked him to get rid of it. He did, I thought.

I also observed my husband noticing other women a lot. He didn't just take a second and third look; he couldn't keep his eyes off them whenever we went anywhere together. One evening we went out to a comedy club together. Throughout the evening when I would glance over at him to share a laugh about a joke, he would be looking at someone at another table, smiling and laughing with her. I was embarrassed and angry. We fought about it. I accused. He denied.

This same kind of interaction happened almost every time we went out together. I was always accusing; he was always denying. Eventually, his words would placate me. I tried to believe him because I wanted it to be true.

Still, I felt the tension. I felt it when we were in public. I felt it when I came home unexpectedly or walked into a room when he was not expecting me. I felt that he was hiding something. I suspected that he still watched pornographic movies behind my back. Periodically, I accused him; he denied it. He felt closed much of the time. We were close, but our relationship lacked real intimacy. We were friends, but our friendship seemed limited. It *was* limited. I just didn't realize how limited it really was.

Then, one warm, summer night, I had to work after hours at an office where I was consulting. My husband was going to stay home and watch TV. Our kids were gone. I left and drove across town, only to find that I didn't have the key to the office with me. Frustrated and impatient, I returned home. I had been gone for about forty-five minutes instead of the expected three hours.

I drove into the garage and hurried into the house to get the key. My husband was standing in the kitchen, looking very tense. I knew I had walked in on something. I don't know how, I just knew.

I walked into the family room and noticed that the blinds on the patio door were closed. I asked him why he had closed the blinds already. He had some excuse. I can't even remember what it was. I walked over to the TV, picked up the remote control and started to turn on the VCR.

He rushed over and grabbed the remote. "You don't want to do that!" he said. "You won't like what you see." He pressed eject, grabbed the tape that came out and broke it in two.

As I began to cry and to question, the whole story came pouring out. Accusations and recriminations followed.

He told me he had been using pornographic videos and magazines to masturbate all through our marriage. He told me that he had a fantasy life that had nothing to do with me. He had a post office box in a little town near ours where he could receive pornographic materials. He used our computer to download pornography. He told me he had tried periodically to change, to quit, but he said he could stop only for a short period of time before he started again. He told me he didn't want to hurt me.

Wave after wave of pain washed over me as he confessed. My response was a mixture of indignation and anger: "Why? How could you? I hate you!" Full knowledge of the extent of his deceit overwhelmed me. I was devastated. The clues, the feelings, the unconscious knowledge were all real.

After more words and more crying, we finally went to bed. I was exhausted and numb. He was cold and defensive. I went to sleep, convinced that our marriage was over.

Coping with the News

People cope with trauma and loss in many different ways. My first coping mechanism was a feeling of numbness. I felt strangely distant from the action.

I experienced shock, pain and anger, yet I felt outside of the experience. I removed myself and stepped out of the nightmare. Then, over the next few days and weeks, I experienced intense anger, feelings of crushing defeat and depression and revenge fantasies. I felt incredibly wronged, that he should pay for the pain he had caused.

I berated myself. *I think I knew. Why didn't I force the issue or leave? Why don't I just leave now? Am I addicted to the addicted? What is wrong with me?*

I searched for answers. *What's really wrong? Why can't he just quit? Why isn't he sexually satisfied by me? How bad is it? Has he told me everything? Can he change? Is he really addicted?*

I struggled. I felt a need for control. I wanted assurance that he wouldn't do this again. I needed some sympathy. I wanted a close friend to confide in, but I didn't really want anyone to know. I felt embarrassed, ashamed, out of control. Your response may be similar or completely different. We all cope with shock in different ways.

My response to this first revelation fell far short of what I have come to know is a better way. At that time, I had been distanced from my faith in God for a period of years. My relationship with Christ had steadily declined over the period of loss I had experienced. I was not fully aware of it as it happened—just a feeling of distance from God. I slowly stopped praying and reading my Bible and finally stopped attending church. At that point, I consciously made a decision to leave it all behind. That was when I met and married my husband.

That night when I caught him, I had been away from church for several years. I had not prayed in a long time. Spiritually, I was in a dry desert. However, God was gracious to me in my despair. He had everything I was struggling for—control, assurance, sympathy, the listening ear. He met me in the desert and gave me water to drink.

A Better Way of Coping

There are many ways to cope with the first revelations of sexual addiction. We all know that some are natural, human ways, while others are less natural and more godly. We cannot control the addiction, but we can control our response. I found a number of ways that worked for me in those first devastating days and in the many months since. Some of these might work for you, some might not.

1. *Read the Bible*. I have found comfort and healing in the Scriptures that I have found nowhere else, even though I have been through many therapy sessions and have read many books. God's Word is living and real. It cuts to the very heart of our need. I have found special comfort in the Psalms. The very heart of God seems to leap out from the verses.

A commitment to read the Bible every day is a commitment to your own health. Please don't read over this and say to yourself, "I've heard that a million times." This is the most important thing you can do for yourself and your marriage. Your heavenly Father is waiting, available and ready to bear your grief. "Praise be to the Lord, to God our Savior, who daily bears our burdens" (Psalm 68:19).

2. Get some distance. As soon as you can, get away for a few days. Even though your impulse might be to stay close and watch, don't! You desperately need physical and emotional relief. There is a perspective that distance alone gives. If it is impossible to leave your work, children and responsibilities, at least take some time away from the house. Get a baby-sitter or take a day off work. When your life is down around your ankles, you can't walk very well. Get away. Get alone. Get going!

3. Make a pros-and-cons list of your options and choices. Amazingly enough, if you sit down by yourself and make a list, you usually find that you have the answers to your problems already. Most of us know what is wrong and what to do to fix it. However, in a crisis, we can be fairly distant from that knowledge. A list will help to bring things back into focus.

Making lists is a constructive step you can take for yourself. I made several lists in the first few weeks following discovery. Here are a couple:

My Options:

1. Stay unconditionally

PROS:

Family stays together
Peace/no more fighting

CONS:

I lose self respect
I have no peace inside
I have to change
No pressure on Paul
    to change

2. Stay conditionally

PROS:

Family together
We have some ground rules
Neither one loses
Peace if we follow ground rules

CONS:

Paul has to change
No guarantees

3. Divorce

PROS:

I have relief

CONS:

Family splits
We are all unhappy
Future would look
    very different

We ended up setting our ground rules together, incorporating the needs each of us felt were important. This was my initial list.

Ground Rules I Need:

1. No more pornography.
2. We get counseling.
3. We go to church together.
4. We find a way to talk about this subject without fighting.

4. Come to an agreement with your spouse on counseling. We started with separate counseling and then progressed to counseling together when that was appropriate. It is my feeling that the dynamics of sexual addiction are deeply rooted in past experience. In my opinion, the spouse needs to have the safety and freedom to explore those dynamics with a counselor alone. However, I believe that there should be a mechanism in place to keep you informed about his progress. I believe also that there is a time when counseling together can be helpful. "The purposes of a man's heart are deep waters, but a man of understanding draws them out" (Proverbs 20:5).

5. Carefully choose someone to confide in. This could be a friend, someone you respect in the church (same sex as you) or a support group. Secrecy is your enemy. Yet you need to be wise in your choice. Choose someone who will support you without condemning your partner. Do not choose someone who will take your side and merely fuel the flames of anger and bitterness. It is good to be heard; it is not good to wallow. Confide, but don't get stuck.

6. Journal. Write down your feelings. There is something about turning our thoughts into written words that is enlightening. It gives us perspective. I found myself replaying situations endlessly in my mind. Many times, writing them down was the only healthy thing for me to do with them. I found that once my thoughts and feelings were on paper, I could let go of them. If you try it, I believe you'll be amazed at the insight you already have.

7. *Pray, pray and pray some more.* I have purposely saved this for last on my list, but not because it is the least important. I believe prayer is the easiest and yet hardest thing to do on this list. We can pray anytime, anywhere. Standing, sitting or kneeling. Silently or out loud. Yet many times when we should, we don't. We wait. We fret. We manipulate and control, only to find that nothing we do works. Then we pray, too late.

I found that when I changed my way of thinking about prayer, it became as natural as breathing or speaking. This great change of attitude was nothing earth-shattering. I simply stopped thinking of prayer as a tenet of the church and a part of my Christian duty. I realized that I didn't *have* to pray; I *could* pray. There was no obligation. I came to see prayer as a great gift sitting on the shelf, with God just waiting for me to use and enjoy it.

When I began to pray earnestly, God heard my prayers and answered them. He opened up amazing insights to me about my husband and myself. Prayer became my lifeline as I wrestled with the destructive forces of addiction that threatened my husband and my marriage.

Prayer is the last on my list, but it should have first priority. All of the previous suggestions should be prefaced with prayer.

The Bible is full of petitions prayed and answered.

> This is the confidence we have in approaching God: that if we ask anything according to his will, he hears us. (1 John 5:14)

> Do not be anxious about anything, but in everything, by prayer and petition, with thanksgiving, present your requests to God. And the peace of God, which transcends all understanding, will guard your hearts and your minds in Christ Jesus. (Philippians 4:6-7)

> For the eyes of the Lord are
>   on the righteous
> and his ears are attentive to
>   their prayer. (1 Peter 3:12)

In the first days after a revelation like this, you feel many different emotions. You alternate between feelings of intense anger, deep pain, even sympathy for the offending partner. It feels like a roller-coaster ride, except there is no metal bar to hang on to through the ride. The Bible says in Hebrews 6:19, "We have this hope as an anchor for the soul, firm and secure. . . ." Hang on to the anchor. You will need hope.

Lying there in bed in the first light of dawn, a thought came. *It's out in the open. Now we can heal.*

Only when it's all out in the open, completely exposed, can a new day dawn in your relationship, in yourself, in your reliance on God. Your days of pain are not over, but at least you know the truth. You know what you're up against. Open the curtains. Let the light in. Let the new day dawn. Face the truth.

Paul Talks . . .

My first experience with pornography happened when I was twelve years old. I found my dad's Playboy *magazines in his closet and borrowed them without his knowledge. Due to my age and the fact that I was somewhat of a loner, its appeal to me was very strong.*

I believe I got hooked for many reasons, partly because I was entering puberty at the time and partly because of my low self-esteem and immaturity. I found a quick fix to temporarily mask my pains, failures and loneliness. I developed a fantasy life that brought instant relief and sexual gratification through masturbation. What I opened up my heart to was guilt, shame and lust.

Temporary gratification I got, but at great emotional cost. Pornography brought my maturation process to a halt. I have since learned that prolonged use of pornography for sexual gratification keeps one's sexual maturity on hold at the level where first encountered.

My strong attraction to pornographic magazines continued until I became a Christian when I was twenty years old. At that time, I experienced a great release from the chains which bound me to pornography, lust and masturbation, but I still failed on rare occasions. I married my first wife when I was an immature twenty-two-year-old. She was eighteen. Six years later it ended in divorce. I take most of the blame for the failure of this marriage due to my immaturity and stubbornness, even though I didn't want the divorce. Our commitment to each other and to God seemed pretty shallow.

In my distress and pain, I sought the quick fix of pornography again with abandon. I turned my back on God and reveled in new highs with the advent of the VCR and video movies. This life of secrecy and self-abuse, both mentally and physically, is a tool of Satan to make a person feel worthless and guilty. It brings about shame, which manifests itself in perpetration of more acts of shame. The one feeds the other in a vicious cycle.

It was through this shame that I felt unable to return to God. I was unworthy, unforgivable. I had such little respect for myself that I felt I would never be able to attract a mate of any value. It was in the midst of this blackness that I met and fell in love with Kathi.

At first, she didn't seem to mind my use of pornography and even joined in with me a few times. When the idea of marriage entered the picture, everything changed. She asked me to stop. I got rid of all my movies and magazines and told her I wouldn't do it again.

Secretly, I felt as though she were being unfair about my use of pornography and that it wasn't hurting anything. I figured if I kept it out of sight and didn't ask her to participate, that should be good enough. I knew one thing very strongly, though: Kathi was a wonderfully loving and nurturing woman I didn't want to lose. I was willing to promise her anything and try to stick with it, if it meant we had a chance.

Neither of us was in a good place spiritually or emotionally. We both were desperately trying to cope with and soothe our own personal wounds. Needless to say, I didn't keep my word. In fact, I was powerless to keep my word. I couldn't believe that I was powerless, nor did I want Kathi to think so, otherwise our marriage was in jeopardy. I didn't want to lose another wife, have another failure.

Kathi was always suspicious, but usually nonconfrontational. I think she felt as though it couldn't hurt her if she didn't see it or hear of it. She stumbled across a video in the VCR one evening when she came home unexpectedly. The curtains were shut and I was acting suspiciously. I had been caught in the act. I thought our marriage was over.

In that moment, all the shame and guilt exploded in me. Feelings ran so deep that at times I felt the only solution was to take myself out of the picture so I couldn't hurt Kathi or any other person again. Two things prevented me from doing just that: my belief in God and my youngest brother's suicide over sexual issues in his life at the age of twenty-eight.

I pleaded with Kathi, but I was also honest about my sexual addiction. "I need help," I told her, "and I'm willing to seek it out." I also told her that I believed that God had the only true healing power. I suggested that we find a church and recommit our lives to Christ. This we did.

Grief and Relief

First Reactions That Really Aren't

There are so many tears to shed. Who would ever know there could be so many, rolling out of my eyes, dripping down my cheeks, dropping to the floor? Is there no end to these raging waters?

Yet, somehow, it feels so good to cry. Some of the pain and rage seems to be flowing out with these tears. I wonder what will be left inside me when all the tears are gone.

FULL KNOWLEDGE OF THE scope of my husband's addiction was a process. It was not complete the first time I caught him, nor the second, nor the third. It was later, several years after the first time, that I learned just how bad it was.

The morning after the first catch, I woke feeling numb. I remembered each confession of the night before. Each one felt like a wound and an affirmation. Dual feelings. Grief and relief. Every word had hurt, but every word had affirmed my inner knowledge. With it out on the table, I had something tangible to deal with at last.

I remember thinking, *I'm not crazy after all. I haven't been imagining. It's all out now. But what do I do now that I know?* There were several options, but I had mixed feelings about what I did and didn't want to do. As I wrestled with this issue, I asked myself what I should do. Should I . . .

. . . use this information against him?

On one hand, I felt a great desire to cause him pain, destroy his "easy life" and move on without him. At the same time, I didn't want to crush him. I loved him. I didn't want to throw all this back in his face. I wanted to comfort him. I knew that I shouldn't want him to hurt and "bleed" as I was.

. . . discourage him to the point of despair?

Again, I wanted him to feel the full force of what he had done to our marriage. I wanted to see despondency on his face, in his movements, and hear it from his lips. I wanted him to give up. If he gave up, I could give up. And yet part of me didn't want to discourage him to the point of despair.

. . . tell someone or keep it secret?

I didn't want anyone to know that we had such a devastating, shameful problem. I was so embarrassed. I felt guilty, that somehow this was my fault. On the other hand, I wanted someone else to know. Sharing it would help me not feel so alone. I felt torn. I didn't want anyone to know how bad he was, but yet I wanted everyone to know so they could sympathize with me.

. . . fall apart emotionally?

I was in agony. I felt I had to take control of my emotions or surely I would explode. At the same time, I just wanted to let go and lose control. I didn't want to shed tears over him and his betrayal, yet I was on the verge of tears most of the time. I felt it was totally unfair that I should not only be the one hurt by his betrayal, but also be the one who had to keep it from spilling over into other parts of our life.

It took me years to figure it all out. How could I feel so relieved one minute and so despairing the next? How could I go on? What was the alternative? Why was I feeling grief? What should I do with it?

A dictionary defines "grief" as: keen mental suffering or distress over affliction or loss; sharp sorrow; painful regret. The same dictionary defines "relief" as: alleviation of or deliverance from pain, distress, anxiety, oppression, etc.

Distress and deliverance. This was my conflict. I felt both in those first few days. I felt both many times throughout the next few years.

Loss of the Dream

As I grew up, I pieced together a picture of what married life should be. From many fragments of relationships, I wove a very pretty pattern of the husband/wife relationship. I envisioned my husband as a caring, sensitive, loving man who would cherish me above all others and share his whole self with me.

I envisioned myself as a loving, caring, sensitive wife who would meet all her husband's needs. I knew problems would arise, but in my dream, we would deal with whatever came up together. We would be one mature, loving team.

It was a beautiful picture of devotion, sharing, friendship and love. But it wasn't real. Not in my first marriage, which ended in my husband's death, and not in my marriage to Paul.

I found out reality is rarely the stuff dreams are made of. I experienced great loss when my first husband died, though our marriage was anything but perfect. In our own ways, we each

had betrayed the other's trust, but we worked
through it. We developed a real relationship and
a slightly modified version of the dream. We
thought we would always be together.

And then he was gone. I grieved his loss, but I
did not give up on the dream. I felt that I was
pretty good at relationships and anticipated another one. With Paul's revelation, however, I
came face-to-face with the loss. Not the loss of
my husband—the loss of my dream. It was un-
avoidable.

I thought, *Here it is. Look at it: the truth. You will
never have what you thought you wanted. Your life is
not the stuff fairy tales are made of. You will not have a
happy ending. You will always have pain.*

According to hospice literature, the loss of our
dreams brings the same or similar reactions as
when we lose a loved one. Here are some of the
common, normal responses to grief:

- A feeling of heaviness in the chest or tightness
  in the throat
- Forgetfulness, a feeling of aimlessness, inabil-
  ity to finish things you start
- An empty feeling in your stomach, loss of ap-
  petite
- Difficulty sleeping, dreams about the loss
- Inability to concentrate, restlessness
- Feeling that the loss isn't real, that it didn't
  happen

- An intense preoccupation with incidents sur-
  rounding the loss
- Crying at unexpected times
- Intense anger at the one who caused the loss

I experienced many of these in the first flush of
loss, yet I had no idea that I was mourning. I certainly did not give myself permission to grieve. I
didn't fully realize what an incredible loss I had
sustained in the erosion of my assumptions. I was
struggling for control. I felt guilty for thinking
some of my thoughts. Thoughts about how much
easier it would be if he just died and how much
happier I would be without him. I was not ready
to share these thoughts with someone else or with
God. I felt so alone.

Eventually, I moved out of my self-imposed iso-
lation and began to grieve my loss in a healthier
way. It took time. It took courage. It took honesty
with counselors and friends and myself. I found
that grief is a healthy response to loss and heart-
ache. It is the only way to really move on. It is
good to grieve.

Here are some ideas about the grieving process
that I have found helpful.

1. Recovery takes time. Loss is painful and traumatic. It takes time to heal. Each person experiences grief differently and at his own pace. As you
are able to acknowledge your loss, you can begin
to move beyond shock, disbelief, numbness and

pain. However, there is no specific, right amount of time that it takes to recover. To "get over it" quickly and "get on with life" is for many a method of avoiding the pain of grief. In reality, this merely prolongs the process. Give yourself time to heal. I still experience times of grief and pain, but I can recognize it now and move through the process more quickly.

   2. *Feeling "crazy" is a normal part of grief.* When a person experiences a major loss, he sometimes feels uncertain and frightened. Panic is a normal by-product of loss. It can cause you to avoid people, want to run away and feel like you are going crazy.

   Feelings of disorganization and confusion are perfectly normal responses to grief. Things you usually take pleasure in may leave you cold. You may feel fatigue and experience a lack of initiative. You might have difficulty going to sleep and lose your appetite. Food might become tasteless.

   If this happens, YOU ARE NOT CRAZY! I was exhausted, had trouble sleeping, couldn't concentrate at work and felt disoriented off and on for several weeks after uncovering Paul's addiction. There were times when my chest hurt and I thought I was having a heart attack. I attended a seminar and couldn't remember where I had parked or even if I had brought my car. I broke down in the parking lot, crying.

   There were times when I thought I was going crazy. There were other times when I was sure of it. I found out these are all normal responses to loss. I wish I had known then.

3. *Guilt and anger are a part of the process.* When loss is experienced, many times people blame themselves. "Maybe this is my fault" can become a recurring theme. If only I had done this, if only I hadn't done that. For me it was "if only I were prettier or thinner or sexier. If only I were a better Christian."

Questioning your responsibility in the events that have happened is normal, but self-reproach is not a healthy road to recovery. You are not to blame for another person's addiction and sin. You are not that powerful. The sooner you embrace this knowledge, the sooner you start to heal.

When you experience a loss, frustration and un-answered questions can cause anger. This ire can be directed at the sinning partner, yourself or God. Sometimes it's all of the above.

The first step in moving beyond your anger is to be able to verbalize it. Expressing how you feel helps to dissipate the pent-up emotion.

There are healthy ways to speak about anger and unhealthy ways. Using "I" messages, such as "I am angry because I am feeling betrayed," is preferable to "you" messages, such as, "You hurt me and I hate you for it!" Or, "How could you do this to me?"

I believe it also helps to express your feelings of resentment and anger to God. I felt bitterness and resentment, but felt ashamed to express it in my prayers. I was also fearful that if I said what I was really feeling, God would give up on me or become angry with me. However, I found that over and over in the book of Psalms, King David cries out to God. He seems to express a whole range of emotions without fear. His trust in the Father seems complete as he makes himself totally vulnerable. He assures us that God hears and cares.

> I cry aloud to the LORD;
>   I lift up my voice to the
>   LORD for mercy.
> I pour out my complaint
>   before him;
>   before him I tell my trouble.
>
> When my spirit grows faint
>   within me,
>   it is you who know my way. . . .
>   (Psalm 142:1-3)

4. Healing takes place when you experience grief. You cannot heal unless you experience and express your grief. Your ability to love again depends on your going through the grieving process. To close yourself off from your feelings is to close the door to a loving relationship. It takes some time and some effort, but if you allow yourself to grieve, you will begin to hope and to heal.

I believe that living with a partner who has a sexual addiction can be even more challenging than the death of a loved one. When you lose a loved one to death, it is incredibly painful but final. With sexual addiction, you may experience loss of trust many times over the course of recovery. I have.

You also may experience the loss of your marriage through divorce. There are times when the marriage is so damaged that it cannot be restored or when the partner is unrepentant. There are also times when the partner is sorry, but unwilling to stop. Whatever the situation, in order for your own health to be restored, you need to grieve your losses. Almost a year after I caught Paul the first time, he made a business trip to Texas. Even though we were attending church and all seemed well, I was full of fear. He didn't call me once while he was gone. When I picked him up at the airport, he seemed a little distant. I didn't know if it was my imagination or if it was real.

I asked him how the weekend went and why he hadn't called. He was defensive. He said the weekend went fine, he had no problems. He hadn't called because he was busy and didn't think there was any need to call unless he had problems.

I became specific in my questioning. "Did you get a magazine?" I asked. We both knew I meant a pornographic magazine.

"No."

"Did you watch a video?" We both knew I meant a pornographic video.

"No," he said. "Some guys had some videos playing in their room, but I didn't watch them."

"Did you go to a topless bar?"

"No."

I didn't believe him, but there was nothing else to say.

A month later, I was watching TV in the living room while Paul was working on the computer. The next day I was going to take a trip to the coast by myself. I was feeling stressed at work and uneasy at home and felt I needed a few days alone.

I got up quickly to pack during a commercial and as I walked by the computer, I caught a glimpse of a woman. I turned around and faced the computer and the screen was empty. I asked Paul what had been on the screen.

He said, "Nothing."

I felt sick. My stomach felt weird and I could hardly breath. I knew. I don't know exactly what I said, but I was so angry I wanted to hurl the computer at him. Instead, I yelled and accused.

Finally, he admitted to downloading some pornographic pictures on a disk and viewing them. I insisted on seeing them.

Slowly, he brought each one onto the screen. After I had seen them all, he took the disk out of the machine and twisted it into pieces. Then we went into the living room and talked.

He admitted to going to a topless bar while in Texas and watching pornographic videos. He said that even though he was trying to live for God and stay away from pornography, nothing seemed to work.

I left the next day for the coast thinking our marriage was indeed over. In the midst of my grief, I wrote:

> Something has always been missing,
>   something has never been there.
> Smoke from burning incense,
>   whirling and curling in air.
> Subtle and wispy fragrance,
>   suggesting that peace could return.
> Gone in less than a heartbeat,
>   as it comes to the end of the burn.
> No substance for me to hang on to,
>   no lingering fragrance to hold.
> Just memories of wisps, and the heartbreak
>   of a room that is suddenly cold.

Poem from Journal

I felt betrayed. I was without much hope for our future, yet was unable to give up. I knew only God could change Paul. I was completely powerless. I spent a couple days alone, walking on the beach, thinking, praying.

I called Paul to see if he had left. He was still there. He said he was sorry and that he wanted to get help. He had contacted our pastor and asked to talk to someone about his addiction. He was hopeful. How could I leave?

Three months later, we went to California for a reunion of Paul's family. I felt tension preparing for the trip. Our relationship was so tenuous, any change seemed like a threat. All went well until the last evening. We were all to go out together to a nightclub. I was apprehensive, but didn't want to be a spoilsport. We went. During the evening, I tried to stay close to Paul; he seemed to be staying close to me.

As we left the club and walked up the street with the family, a woman got out of a car at the curb. Paul looked at her, looked away, then looked again and kept looking for what seemed like a long time to me. It was really just a matter of seconds. We got into our car to go to Paul's sister's house to spend the night and I confronted him.

He said, yes, he had looked at her, and yes, he had looked twice.

I asked him why and he said, "Because I wanted to see her better."

I was crushed and felt total despair. I asked him to take me to the airport.

He said, "No."

I told him I was fed up with his faithless heart and I was leaving him.

When we got to his sister's house, Paul went in and told the family we were having problems and I would not be staying the night there. His dad and stepmother offered to take me home with them. I went.

The next day, Paul went back to Oregon and I stayed in California. He made a decision to seek professional help from a Christian counselor. I made a decision to stay with him and see if it would help.

Paul Talks . . .

When we started going back to church, the rate of my pornographic use diminished significantly. However, the degree of guilt and shame increased dramatically. Now, when I lied to Kathi, I was lying to God also.

Accusations usually surrounded my roving eyes when we were in public and suspicion of what I was doing in private. Because of this, in our sixth year of marriage, she left me for about a week. This was devastating. I thought I'd lost her. I pled with Kathi again and promised I'd do anything to keep her. Whatever it took, I'd do it.

When she returned, I went to a Christian counselor who worked extensively in the field of sexual addiction. He gave me numerous personality tests, as well as two lie detector tests. I also dutifully went to a twelve-step program for sexual addiction. After a year, I quit. I found it very difficult to deal with a group of individuals who would admit their problems, but who wouldn't admit that God had the power to change them. The only support was supposed to come from being able to unload within a safe group of people who had similar problems.

They talked about a higher power, which could be anything, including a stuffed teddy bear. To this "power" they gave the credit for their faithfulness, but then would have to admit failure again and again. It seemed to me they really had no hope and couldn't offer any. I know this system has benefits and works for some people, but I was frustrated because I felt God was missing from the formula.

The counselor had me read numerous books on sexual addiction. While under this magnifying glass, I managed to avoid pornography. My spiritual growth, however, was still stagnant and without conviction.

We Have Today . . . or Do We?

Living Intimately with Distrust

I feel like I'm losing ground, doing hand-to-hand combat with fear. This is a fight I can't win. I feel paralyzed by emotions, fears and feelings. I'm so depressed and so miserable. I feel like I'm going down, sinking fast.

TRUST WAS ONE OF the first casualties in my relationship with my husband. My trust in him was tenuous to begin with. I did not feel that he would necessarily be with me for the rest of my life. I wasn't sure if I could count on him for the long haul.

The problem wasn't all his by any means. I came into the relationship with some well entrenched insecurities of my own. My father had been gone for most of my childhood. He was in prison from the time I was two years of age until I was nine. I spent those seven years of my early childhood feeling very lonely for my dad.

My father died when I was twenty-nine. This time, he was gone for good and I felt inconsolable with his loss. I remember vividly what happened when I heard of his death. I was up late after the children were put to bed, mopping my kitchen floor. In those days with three little boys, that might be the only time I had for housecleaning.

The phone rang and it was a friend of my brother calling from Oregon. My parents were out there visiting my brother at the time. She told me my father had been rushed to the hospital with a massive coronary and he was not expected to live.

I barely heard the details. When she hung up, I started to finish the mopping and I began to cry. Down on my hands and knees, in the middle of the floor, I mourned. I wailed, moaned, with deep convulsive cries of agony. I knew he was gone and would never be back. I was cut off, my connection to history lost. I grieved for a short period of time and then swallowed it to console my mother. I needed to be strong for her.

Then four years later my first husband died. This death was not as much of a shock, simply because we knew he had cancer and had a year to prepare. However, it was no less agonizing. Again I felt cut off, this time from the present. All that I had assumed about my life was gone. I needed to be strong. I had children to take care of, bills to pay, a job to go back to.

I had been a Christian since the age of twelve and God was the source of my security. However, my grip on my relationship with Him began to loosen. Trusting got harder. Being strong got easier. My children, my friends and my work became my sources of security.

I tried to be a good mother, a devoted friend and a skilled business manager. Keeping things under control seemed the only safe thing to do. My spiritual life was put on hold. I wrote in my journal:

If things were always just the way I thought they should be, would I be bored out of my mind or somehow set free from brooding about what isn't and what is and longing for control?

Journal Entry

When I met Paul, I was at an all time high in self-confidence about my abilities and my appearance. It didn't take long to lose it. As revelation after revelation came about his use of pornography, I began comparing myself to other women.

I felt he was making constant comparisons also, and there was no way I could measure up. Feelings of rejection and low self-esteem grew. I became miserably insecure with my husband.

At times, the weight of my self-doubt became unbearable, incredibly oppressive, unalterable. Doing well at work helped. Being a good mother helped. Having friends helped. But at the heart of my life, in my most intimate relationship, I was miserable and insecure.

This feeling of inadequacy is a crushing weight to carry. If only I were beautiful. If only I had a better body. If only he could actually see me. I'm not that bad. I think I'm a pretty good package. I shouldn't beat myself up for what I'm not. If only he had a faithful heart.

Journal Entry

I came to believe that I was not the girl of his dreams and never would be. I know now that even if I were, it wouldn't make any difference. He often tells me I am everything he wanted. He points out all the things that I am—a good mother, a faithful wife, a hard worker, a joyful companion with a good sense of humor, smart, responsible, stable, caring, loving, physically attractive to him, and the list goes on. But the reality is, I am reality. And it isn't reality that he is addicted to.

Throughout our marriage, I tried with varying degrees of success to be what he wanted. When we got married, I was thin. I had been thin for most of my adult life. I worked at it, and I liked the results. The men in my life seemed to think I was attractive also. That is, until I met Paul.

From the start, he said I was too thin. I needed to gain some weight. I was amazed and, quite frankly, pleased. I could relax a little and put on a few pounds and my husband would actually be happier.

When I asked him why, he said if I put on some weight, maybe my breasts would grow. I was pretty small. No one in their wildest dreams would have used the word "buxom" in connection with me.

So I gained weight, about twenty pounds, in the next five years. Once in a while, he mentioned breast augmentation as a possibility. It was kind of a joke. I felt that if I were to have cosmetic surgery, it sure wouldn't be breast enlargement. We left it at that, but my low self-esteem kicked in and I thought, *I am not enough. I'll never be enough.*

Cosmetic surgery would have made very little difference. I would still have been reality, a living, breathing person with strengths and weaknesses— day to day the same.

In marriage, two people become intimately acquainted with each other. They know each other almost as well as they know themselves. You live your life with that person. Each day of sharing life, with all its ups and downs, cements the relationship into a whole lifetime of shared memories.

I believe that was what my husband wanted most deeply, and yet, the sameness of one partner for life stifled him. He chose many years before I came into his life to augment reality with fantasy. It was impossible for me to compete with those fantasies.

Pornographic magazines and videos, even affairs with other women, never become ordinary, familiar, everyday. There is always the element of excitement, the touched-up, airbrushed, film-clipped element of fantasy. There is always the element of the forbidden, the glimpse of something enticing, the lure of sin. A mere living, breathing mate cannot compete on any level.

For a while, I tried. I gained the weight. I tried to be sexier than I felt. Nothing I did changed what he did. I did not trust him; he was not trustworthy.

My husband's growth in this area has been a process. He did not just turn his back on everything at once. He made commitments to not purchase magazines or rent pornographic movies. However, he allowed himself the freedom to look at magazines with scantily clad women and to rent explicit R-rated films.

Then, he committed to not purposefully *looking* at explicit magazines and not renting R-rated videos. However, he allowed himself the freedom to linger over *covers* of explicit videos and magazines and he always allowed himself the freedom of looking at and watching other women in public places.

He has grown now to the point of feeling that his decision to purposefully view things that sexually excite him is sin. He has not always kept his commitments, but he is working on it. It is a process.

Why did I pick someone who was so inaccessible, someone I couldn't trust? Why did I attach to this person who wants something I'm not? How in the world can I ever trust him again? I can't just speak trust into existence, can I?

Journal Entry

I spent several years in the darkness of distrust. I struggled with it yesterday and I struggle with it today.

I am not proud of some of the things I did under the influence of distrust. I watched every move Paul made, even after he was in counseling and seemed to be doing well. Always, on some level, I was noticing, looking for signs of a relapse. I felt tied to him— like I couldn't leave him for any length of time. I questioned him, asking the same questions five ways, hoping for a clue to the truth.

He worked at home during these years and I was the executive director of a Christian organization. I would come home from work and begin:

"How was your day?"

"Fine."

"Did you have any problems?"

"No."

"Did you watch TV?"

"No."

"Did you get a video?"

"No."

"Did you look at anything you shouldn't?"

"No."

"Would I think you had a good day?"

"Yes."

"Did you masturbate?"

"No. Will you please stop!"

I did not believe any of his answers. I imagined things he was probably doing behind my back. These scenarios became as real and as hurtful as the truth that I knew. I kept going back to those places of inferiority and pain in my mind, mulling them over, trying to fix them.

I found that lack of trust tied me to my husband's every move. I searched for hidden pornographic magazines and video tapes when he wasn't home. I searched his car, his shop, his dresser and his pockets. I checked the garbage can. I looked in empty boxes and luggage. I watched the receipts from the grocery store.

I never found any hidden pornography by searching for it. I only seemed to find it when I wasn't searching.

What I did find was that I was totally focused on my husband and his addiction. There was no room for trust. I found that searching and checking up and watching took an enormous amount of energy. It was exhausting. I found that what you dwell on, you become. I became obsessed with his addiction, hypersensitive to his every move. He hated the scrutiny.

I was so mixed up, I couldn't even begin to think about trust. I needed to let God have the rightful place of leadership in my life, to find again my security in his great, immeasurable love for me. I needed to pry this problem out of my tightly clenched fist and give it to God. That felt pretty dangerous. To just let go of it somehow seemed impossible. Here is a journal entry from that time which shows where I was in my thinking.

Here you are, old friend, the longing, the empty need to be filled. The inside of my insides longs for peace and soothing tenderness. It is nowhere to be found. There is no balm for the longing, no healing for the heart.

Journal Entry

I was raw, exposed and empty. The distrust I felt was not limited to my husband. The very core of it lay in my lack of trust in God. It wasn't until I began to trust God for my strength and my well-being that I was able to let go of my obsession with my husband's addiction and move into a more trusting relationship with him. This was such a slow process.

I don't know exactly when I came to the realization that I needed to change. It wasn't some simple little plan, no easy steps—one, two, three and you're there. It was slow and painstaking and I resisted mightily the idea that I needed to change.

But change happened over time. I took specific steps, and from this vantage point, I can put them together in a fairly sensible form. While these are the things I did, you might not need to take these steps or you might have others that you need to take instead. Each situation is different.

Steps to a More Trusting Relationship

A dictionary defines "trust" as "reliance on the integrity, strength, ability, surety, etc., of a person or thing; confidence." I believe the very first steps you must take have nothing to do with your mate and his trustworthiness—mine wasn't trustworthy so how could I trust him? Rather, they have to do with your relationship with God, your Father, your closest, most important relationship.

1. I needed to trust in my salvation.

> Know therefore that the LORD your God is God; he is the faithful God, keeping his covenant of love to a thousand generations of those who love him and keep his commands. (Deuteronomy 7:9)

Wow, this sounds like a God who keeps His promises. How novel.

If we confess our sins, he is faithful and
just and will forgive us our sins and purify
us from all unrighteousness. (1 John 1:9)

I had confessed. I had been cleansed. I had for-
gotten, but now my memory was refreshed.

For I am convinced that neither death nor
life, neither angels nor demons, neither the
present nor the future, nor any powers,
neither height nor depth, nor anything else
in all creation, will be able to separate us
from the love of God that is in Christ Jesus
our Lord. (Romans 8:38-39)

Nothing could separate me but me. There were
many periods when I had no assurance of anything but my own strength. I had lost the confidence that is in Christ. Since I had lost it, I had to
find it. It was no one else's fault. Not my husband's, not the pornographer's, not an inept counselor or a less-than-supportive church. It was
mine.

2. *I needed to trust in God's ability to redeem and
transform.*

"I have told you these things, so that in me
you may have peace. In this world you will
have trouble. But take heart! I have overcome the world." (John 16:33)

> Therefore he is able to save completely those who come to God through him, because he always lives to intercede for them. (Hebrews 7:25)

> I have swept away your offenses like a cloud, your sins like the morning mist. Return to me, for I have redeemed you. (Isaiah 44:22)

Oh boy—peace in tribulation, courage, saved forever, redeemed—this did not sound like my life. I did not have much peace; I had little or no courage. I did not feel safe or saved very often and I didn't have a handle on redeemed. I had to go all the way back to take hold of His promises for myself, to put my name in and claim them for me. I had to stop trying to do it on my own.

Driving home from a ladies' meeting, I stopped my car and wrote . . .

It is hard to let go. God, You have to change me. Will You? I can't, I've tried. I can't do this. I cannot do "struggling, conquering, having the victory." It's not going to happen. You will have to change me. I must let it go. Here it is. Please teach me to surrender it all. Please!

Journal Entry

With the relinquishment of my control, peace came. Courage started to grow and I knew I was saved no matter what. Then came the realization that God could take the worst failures of my life and turn them into the greatest blessings.

I listened to a tape a friend had sent me of a pastor's wife talking about this very thing. She spoke of failure and loss and how God can take our worst failures and turn them into something useful and worthwhile. I was deeply moved to realize that God could and would use my failures, if I would just let go of them.

3. *I needed to trust in God's plan for my life.*

"For I know the plans I have for you," declares the LORD, "plans to prosper you and not to harm you, plans to give you hope and a future." (Jeremiah 29:11)

A friend of mine quoted this verse several times to me before I got it. I just kept hearing it and applying it to her. In the face of such an overwhelming promise, I doubted. I totally dismissed and denied that there could be a plan in all this. My plan was all I wanted. I knew I had not asked for this pain. I certainly had not planned it, wouldn't ever have planned it and didn't want it. I could not see any positive use in it at all and yet here was the promise.

Then in my Bible study, I read, "God is not a man, that he should lie, nor a son of man, that he should change his mind. Does he speak and then not act? Does he promise and not fulfill?" (Numbers 23:19).

Suddenly it hit me. I had been treating God like a human. People lie, people change their minds, people don't always keep their promises. But God is not a human being. I can trust Him. God does have a plan for my life. If I just relinquish the controls and relax, He can work that plan. He has promised that His plans for me are far better than any I could ever dream or devise.

Through the changes God has wrought, I now believe I can trust God's plan for both my life and my husband's. Living on the edge of my seat, ready to stand up and take control, is not the plan. I believe that developing trust is an exercise for yourself, not the other person. However, you will both reap the blessings and benefits.

Take action to trust. Deny mistrust a foothold. I am not saying you should be blind, but don't see every action through the lens of suspicion, as I did. Do not deny your feelings or ignore real signs of trouble. Keep yourself healthy. Don't let distrust eat away your joy. This is not a "don't worry, be happy" philosophy of living. This is a call to take possession of your right to joy in the Lord and to take hold of the promise of a sound mind. You can trust God! "For God did not give us a spirit of timidity [fear, in the KJV], but a spirit of power, of love and of self-discipline" (2 Timothy 1:7).

Suspicion and mistrust are twin deceivers, robbers, thieves of joy. A good friend and counselor used the following illustration when discussing mistrust and suspicion with me: When you are suspicious, you put a noose around the neck of the person you do not trust. The other end of the rope is in your own hand. As long as you are suspicious, you remain tied completely, inexorably to the very person you mistrust. You not only deny that person freedom, you deny yourself freedom.

He said, "Kathi, take the noose of suspicion off of his neck. Let go of it."

I try to visualize the rope in my hand, pulling on his neck when I start feeling suspicious. Sometimes, I actually see myself let go of the rope. Those are moments of great release.

If you plant suspicion, you reap mistrust. If you plant trust, you reap contentment, peace and joy. Suspicion takes an incredible amount of energy. It is exhausting. Trusting takes much less energy. It is energizing.

The exhausting cycle of my suspicion went something like this:

Suspicion: I saw him linger too long looking at someone or something, or I got a feeling that things were not as they seemed.

Questioning: I asked him questions over and over. Same question, several different ways. "Did you buy a magazine? Did you see a magazine? Did you find a magazine and look through it? Do you have a magazine hidden? Do you have anything hidden?"

Mistrust: I doubted his explanations and answers to my questions. I imagined what could be going on behind my back.

Pain: I felt extreme hurt and pain for past wrongs and what I thought might be happening now.

Anger: Feelings of hurt and pain gave place to intense anger for being wronged over and over again. I withdrew any feelings of tenderness I felt toward him.

Bitterness: Feelings of anger became entrenched. I felt hatred and bitterness toward him, so much so that at times, I couldn't see any good in him. I wanted to punish him. I wanted him to pay for my pain.

Shame: Then I felt so ashamed of my thoughts, so distant from God. I wondered if I were crazy. Was I just imagining he was in the cycle again or was it for real? I also felt disappointed in myself for giving in to suspicion.

Then it started all over again. This cycle keeps your heart locked up. When you are a prisoner of distrust, you are so focused on your own self and your own needs that you cannot be the kind of mother, friend and wife you want to be. All you can think of is getting out of that cold, dark place. I hated it there, and yet I had the keys right in my own hand all the time. I could get out of the cycle without my husband's help. I could take responsibility for my own release from distrust and suspicion. I could trust God.

Rebuilding Trust

There are some things you can do to help rebuild trust in your partner. Here are a few we have tried. Sometimes one will help, sometimes another will.

1. Take note of the little victories, both yours and his. When I first became aware of the extent of my husband's addiction, I thought if he wanted to and he really tried, he could just stop doing the things that hurt us both. In reality, he couldn't and neither could I. I couldn't just stop my own destructive cycle of suspicion and speak trust into existence. And he couldn't just cease to look at or long for another piece of pornography. We both had to give our separate sins to the Lord and begin to rely on Him for our strength.

We also needed to open our eyes to the little victories we were each having. When I started seeing his little achievements, such as turning his head away when we passed seductive magazines in the supermarket, my trust began to grow and I was able to say, "Thanks, I really appreciate that." He, in turn, appreciated my noticing his victories and felt less defeated and responsible for hurting me.

2. Rest in what your partner is doing right. My husband did so many things right. He was thoughtful, never picked me apart in public, rarely criticized me. He was kind and very loving. He was intelligent, humorous and usually approachable. We shared many of the same likes and dislikes, many of the same goals in life. He loved my children. He did kind things for me—making my coffee in the morning, running my bath, making sure I took my vitamins.

In my own mind, though, there was always a "but." "Yes, he is nice, but . . . ." As I began to notice his wonderful parts and stopped adding "but" to every positive thought about him, I was able to get a better perspective. There were some things about him that *were* trustworthy.

Here is a positive exercise you can do. Read Philippians 4:8 and ask God to open your eyes to good things about your mate and to give you renewed desire to think about these good points. It really did help me. It might help you!

> Finally, brothers, whatever is true, whatever is noble, whatever is right, whatever is pure, whatever is lovely, whatever is admirable—if anything is excellent or praiseworthy—think about such things.

3. Don't dwell on suspicious circumstances. There are always going to be circumstances that come up that don't look good. Scrutinizing a person's every action is bound to dredge up some things that look really bad, at least on the surface.

When I watched Paul's every move, I found myself accusing him a lot. Sometimes he didn't have a clue what I was talking about. Be careful of

your words; they are powerful. By dwelling on
suspicious circumstances, you can discourage your
mate and assist in his failure.

Certainly there are times when you need to ask
him questions and talk about things that look suspicious to you. You should feel free to do that, but
don't let your mind dwell on suspicions. Don't
give them room to grow. Get rid of them. You can
pray immediately and ask God to take care of a
suspicious circumstance and give you peace. I love
the two verses in the Philippians 4 passage that
read:

> Do not be anxious about anything, but in
> everything, by prayer and petition, with
> thanksgiving, present your requests to
> God. And the peace of God, which tran-
> scends all understanding, will guard your
> hearts and your minds in Christ Jesus.
> (Philippians 4:6-7)

What a promise! My ability to lay my suspicions and this problem at God's feet varies
greatly. Sometimes I am at peace, other times,
not.

As I waffle, time and again the Holy Spirit
brings to mind the Scripture, "You will keep in
perfect peace him whose mind is steadfast, because he trusts in you" (Isaiah 26:3). When I trust
the Lord, my feelings of inadequacy, fear and
loneliness seem to fade and I feel like a big puzzle
whose pieces are all drawn into their respective

places by an unseen magnet. I feel whole and safe, able to meet and actually welcome each new day. When I give in to my doubts, I'm afraid of what the day might bring.

Establishing trust has been a very hard discipline for me. I'm not there yet. I don't always take control of my thoughts and pray immediately. But I'm learning. I'm gaining strength as I practice these Scriptures. I know I can't always trust my husband, and I can't necessarily trust myself. However, I know I can trust God. A verse in Isaiah puts this all in perspective for me. "Stop trusting in man, who has but a breath in his nostrils. Of what account is he?" (2:22).

The alternative is not pretty, as the following entry from my journal bears out.

Checking him out. Laying some traps. I'm the one feeling trapped. On some level, I know that he is going to hurt me again. In the abyss of my anger and suspicion, I feel a cool hand on my arm, a little voice in my heart, encouraging me to take charge of my reaction, make a different choice—the choice of peace.

Journal Entry

Paul Talks . . .

Our spiritual growth was slow. My use of pornography continued off and on, as did Kathi's suspicions and accusations. Being in public became torture for both of us, but especially for Kathi. If she didn't see me noticing another woman, she imagined it. Sometimes, she saw another woman before me and watched to see if I noticed her.

She continually accused me of using pornography secretly. She assumed that if I couldn't control myself in public, I must be doing other things in private. This was far from the truth, but her fears were very real and torturing.

We had these heated confrontations where she accused me and I denied looking at so-and-so at such-and-such a time. We both walked away from these battles angry, with nothing resolved.

I felt she didn't understand the nature of men and that she was being unfair in her demands and suspicions. She felt as though I were being unfaithful and lying. The truth was somewhere in between.

It is natural for men to notice attractive women. Unfortunately, in our society, it is acceptable for women to display their sexuality very openly in public. This intensifies the Christian man's predicament of where to draw the line.

I still wrestle with this issue, but I am much clearer on the point at which I am sinning. If, when I notice a woman, I begin to have any thoughts that are other than wholesome and entertain them, I am sinning. If I have a hard time taking my eyes off another woman or I find myself looking several times, again I am sinning.

When this happens, the right response for me is to tell my wife I'm sorry and to put my eyes back on God. I don't always do it, but I'm getting better.

Forgiving, Forgiving, Forgiving

Can I?
Why Should I?

I thought we were past this kind of relapse. I was wrong. All the way back. I feel so numb and unbelieving. Not that same devastating hurt and anger, more of a dull pain and a sense of despair. Knowing this will never end; wondering how long I'm expected to endure it and forgive. On some level, knowing the answer to that question. Forgiving doesn't have a limit.

For several days, though, I have bounced back and forth between leaving and staying, even going so far as writing a list of what I will need to take when I go. He alternates between remorse and his own anger at the idea that I would leave him. Also, dealing with his own sense of betrayal and knowing that he cannot trust himself. There seems to be no stopping this insatiable need. I am close to giving up.

THE YEARS SPENT WORKING in a Christian organization were years of growth and rebuilding in my relationship with Paul. He attended a Christian college in the evenings to obtain a degree in management and developed a home business. We were active in church. Our relationship started feeling very solid.

Our business grew to the point that my skills were needed. We thought the income could sustain us, so I left the nonprofit ministry and became self-employed. We made a business move to Arizona and all seemed well. Both of us saw this as a new start—new house, new town, no old memories. However, we had difficulty getting connected with a new church.

In the spring, Paul decided he wanted to attend a Promise Keepers meeting in Los Angeles. I was very happy. On the bus, he met some men from a church in our town, a place we had not yet attended. When he came home, he said he would like to visit this new church. I was happy to comply, glad that he had made a connection.

We began attending and immediately felt welcomed. Very quickly, we developed relationships with several families. We attended a midweek growth group and Sunday services when possible; our business required us to be out of town on weekends a lot. I was feeling better and better about our marriage.

Then in July, we took a business trip in our RV.
Before the trip, Paul suggested we get some movies to take along for entertainment. We had a small
TV we sometimes took with us in our motor-
home. I thought that sounded great. We'd have
something to do in the evenings besides playing
games, as was our custom.

On the trip, I thought I noticed Paul eyeing
women when we stopped. I wasn't sure, but I began
to feel suspicious. However, we were reading a book
on men's sexuality, written by a popular Christian
author, and discussing it openly. Paul didn't seem to
be hiding anything and we were praying together,
so I thought maybe it was just me.

One evening, we stopped in a little town for the
night and noticed a movie playing at a theater that
we thought we'd like to see. I needed to make a call
to our son, who was in college, and wanted to shop
in a little antique store we had driven by. We parked
the RV and Paul said he was tired and wanted to
rest for a little while before we went to the movie.
He suggested I go make the call and do my shopping and then we could eat and go to the movie.

I thought, *Yes! I can take my time looking at an-
tiques.* I decided to make my call first. I went to a
phone booth and placed the call. Our son was not
home so I left a message on his answering machine
and proceeded to do some serious shopping.

As I walked into the little shop, the clerk said,
"I'm sorry, we're closing." I was so disappointed. I
walked back to the RV. I had only been gone
about fifteen minutes.

I reached for the door handle. It was locked, so I knocked. I was not suspicious, because I expected Paul to lock it when he took a nap in a strange town. It took Paul a few minutes to open it. When I looked at his face, I knew. I asked him what was the matter.

He said nothing.

The TV was sitting out on the bed.

I asked him what he had been doing. He said he had decided to see if he could catch the local weather report.

I walked over to the TV, which had a built in videotape player and started to turn it on. It was the same song, second verse.

He said, "You don't want to do that."

I said, "Why not?"

"Because I have a *Playboy* videotape," he said.

I was in total shock. I knew Paul still struggled, but I was confident he was winning. I was so wrong.

That night was very long. I cried some, but mostly I was just numb. I felt totally hopeless. So did he. There weren't a lot of words to say. I thought about our friends at church, our sons, our families. How hard it would be to tell them all we were divorcing and why. I tried to visualize leaving. *What would I take? Where would I go?*

Somehow, we made it through the night and the next few days. I know we were both praying, neither one of us feeling at all hopeful.

At some point on the trip, Paul said he wanted to go to a counselor in the church. He asked if there was any way I would stay until after he went. He said this was his only hope and even if I left, he would go.

I made the decision to stay. I didn't have anything to lose; I'd already lost it.

When Paul left for the appointment, he was apprehensive and tense. When he came home from the appointment, I was amazed. He looked peaceful, happy and hopeful. I couldn't believe it. He asked me if I would take a walk with him. That was about the last thing I wanted to do, but I said, "Yes."

On the walk, Paul shared with me what had happened. He had expected stern rebuke and had received, instead, loving support. He had expected counsel on how he should leave pornography alone and had instead received counsel on how he could receive forgiveness. He had gone feeling guilty, ashamed and condemned and instead came back feeling clean and forgiven. He had gone with little hope and instead came back full of hope that with God's strength he could win this deadly battle for his soul.

I responded to his sense of hope. I committed to stay with him for six months to see if this was real.

However, I was a long way from forgiving. Nowhere near. Not even close.

I asked myself, *How can a person forgive and forgive and forgive the same wrong? Is it possible? If it is possible, why should I make the effort? At some point, don't I have a right to stop forgiving? After all, I'll probably just have to do it again.* I was feeling very injured, very much in need of some sympathy.

Forgiveness has never come easy for me. Though I was not conscious of it, I practiced what I now call "selective forgiveness." Sometimes, if I

didn't feel too hurt, I would forgive. Then other ·
times, when I felt devastated, I would not forgive.
When this happened, I stored the hurt and anger
deep inside. Then when another hurtful incident
happened, I not only felt bad about that, but I remembered those incidents I had stored away and
my hurt and anger intensified.

I knew I could choose to forgive, but I thought,
Why should I? I felt so wronged. If I forgave fully, he
would be totally off the hook. If I didn't take some revenge myself, he would go completely free. And I
didn't want that. I wanted him to pay! Pay for caring
more about himself than about me! Pay for my pain!

I knew it wasn't over. It would happen again
and again and again. He had confessed, was re-
morseful and was getting help. But it would happen again. Once more, I would be called on to
forgive. This seemed outrageous to me. What justice was there in this situation? How many times
would I have to go through this?

I joined a ladies' Bible study shortly after Paul
started counseling again. One morning, a beautiful
young woman got up and read a letter she had
written to her father. She was a victim of incest
and her letter was one of forgiveness. I was
touched by her forgiving love, which was ex-
pressed so beautifully in her letter, and I was con-
victed about my own lack of forgiveness.

She said she had struggled for a while with fear
and anger and an inability to forgive. Then a Christian friend told her to decide to forgive and pray for
God's help to do it. God answered her prayer.

I decided then and there if she could forgive something so painful and debilitating, I could surely forgive Paul. With my decision and through my prayers, I began to get the right perspective on forgiveness. The Lord also enabled me to let go of my natural desire for justice. Still even then, even now, it was hard to practice forgiveness.

Without Christ, there could be no forgiving, no ability to keep on in this relationship. In the light of His all-encompassing forgiveness, Paul's indebtedness to me began to pale into insignificance. My desire to hold on to bitterness was exposed for what it was—sin.

I found the Bible to be full of teaching on forgiveness. Probably the most well-known text is in Matthew.

> Then Peter came to Jesus and asked, "Lord, how many times shall I forgive my brother when he sins against me? Up to seven times?"
>
> Jesus answered, "I tell you, not seven times, but seventy-seven times." (Matthew 18:21-22)

Then Jesus went on to tell a story about an unmerciful servant who was forgiven a great debt, but who would not forgive a small debt owed to him. This servant ended up in jail to be tortured until he paid back every cent he owed because he was unmerciful.

Jesus ended the teaching with these words: "This is how my heavenly Father will treat each of you unless you forgive your brother from your heart" (18:35).

In reading this passage, I came face-to-face with the knowledge that I was the unmerciful servant. As I began to work on my unforgiving heart, I began to see a theme emerging from Scripture: Forgive because you have been forgiven. That's it. There isn't any other option or any circumstance when not forgiving is justified.

There are many Scriptures on forgiveness, but I have listed only a few. They continue to help me. I hope they will benefit you as well.

> Therefore, as God's chosen people, holy and dearly loved, clothe yourselves with compassion, kindness, humility, gentleness and patience. Bear with each other and forgive whatever grievances you may have against one another. Forgive as the Lord forgave you. (Colossians 3:12-13)

> Be kind and compassionate to one another, forgiving each other, just as in Christ God forgave you. (Ephesians 4:32)

> You are forgiving and good, O Lord,
>   abounding in love to all who call to you.
>   (Psalm 86:5)

Can a person forgive again and again? The answer is an emphatic and resounding, "YES!" The question is how? It takes work. Here are some things you can do.

1. Remember that you yourself are totally, continually forgiven.

> The LORD is compassionate
>   and gracious,
>   slow to anger, abounding in love.
>
> . . . .
>
> he does not treat us as our
>   sins deserve
>   or repay us according to our
>   iniquities.
>
> . . . .
>
> as far as the east is from the
>   west,
>   so far has he removed our
>   transgressions from us.
>   (Psalm 103:8, 10, 12)

Therefore, there is now no condemnation for those who are in Christ Jesus. (Romans 8:1)

Here is God, the Ultimate Example, modeling "forgiveness that forgets," the kind that doesn't even remember the incident. Has no recollection of it. Has erased it. When we are in Christ, we have forgiveness that we absolutely do not deserve, an incredible continuing forgiveness.

It is hard for me to grasp this concept, this reality. It seems so unnatural. And it is. In comparison, my desire to hold on to the hurts, to withhold my forgiveness seems very petty. Natural and understandable, maybe, but petty. How can I not forgive in the light of His daily forgiveness?

2. Acknowledge and mourn the loss of dreams. We all enter marriage with certain dreams about what that marriage will be like. Many of us long for a sensitive, supportive, loving husband. We sometimes have very unrealistic ideas about living happily ever after. When we are betrayed in this closest of relationships, we suffer loss, the disintegration of our dreams. Part of being able to forgive is being able to mourn this loss. Don't just go on with life and stuff it. Realize that something has been taken from you and that it is healthy to grieve the loss. It seems I have to do this with each new incident of betrayal. Recurring loss calls for recurring grief.

3. Take action to forgive. A dictionary defines "forgiveness" as: the act of pardon or remission, absolving; to cease to feel resentment against. Forgiveness is an action. It is not a feeling. However, in time, the feeling of forgiveness follows the action of forgiveness.

It is very difficult to let go of our right to justice, especially when we know that we will probably have to forgive and forgive and forgive again.

It is easy to become consumed with "what he did
to me." Being consumed with wrongs that we
have suffered will eventually consume us. Bitterness can lead to strokes, high blood pressure, even
cancer.

When we decide to forgive, we begin to release our own pain. We decide to give it up and
let it go. In the beginning, I felt forgiveness was
somehow passive and weak. Now I realize forgiveness takes strength and determination and is,
in fact, a very powerful act. Never easy, but
powerful and healing!

4. Pray for an increased ability to forgive. John gave
some powerful promises in his first epistle:

> This is the confidence we have in ap-
> proaching God: that if we ask anything ac-
> cording to his will, he hears us. And if we
> know that he hears us—whatever we ask—
> we know that we have what we asked of
> him. (1 John 5:14-15)

If we ask God to help us forgive, He will. Many
times, I struggled with asking God for help in this
area. I felt so wronged. Deep down I wanted to
hold on to a little part of unforgiveness. However,
when I started praying earnestly for a forgiving
heart, God was quick to answer my prayers. Little
by little, my capacity to forgive seemed to grow.
One of my journal entries reads:

Forgiveness and love
*   take hold of the strong hand of hope*
*   and dance the soothing waltz of peace—*
One, two, three
One, two, three,
I love him, he loves me,
I love him, he loves me ...

Journal Entry

I have learned to pray not just for the ability to forgive current and past wrongs, but for an expanded ability to forgive future wrongs as many times as they come. For me, this was not easy. I got so tired of having to forgive. Many times, I felt worn down, unable to forgive one more thing. I sure didn't want to pray about additional wrongs. But God keeps His promises. He is faithful. If you ask Him to increase your ability to fully forgive, believing that He will answer, He will. I know, because He has.

5. *Don't keep count; let it go.* It is my nature to want to go over everything. I want to talk about it, relive it, plumb the depths of it. In order to forgive, I had to stop rehashing and reliving all the wrongs. I could not just erase all the memories, but I could choose not to relive them.

If we have the same anger, pain, fear and feeling of betrayal when our memories surface as we did when the betrayal took place, we probably have not forgiven. As we forgive, those memories lose their intensity and power to debilitate us. If we

hoard our hurts, they will weigh us down and
eventually take us down.

We can take action to let go of our hurts. I
sometimes visualize taking the pain that I'm feeling and putting it into God's big hands. It feels
so good to get rid of it.

> Brothers, I do not consider myself yet to
> have taken hold of it. But one thing I do:
> Forgetting what is behind and straining to-
> ward what is ahead, I press on toward the
> goal to win the prize for which God has
> called me heavenward in Christ Jesus.
> (Philippians 3:13-14)

6. Don't give the advantage to Satan. For a time, I
felt my hatred and bitterness were totally justified. I had been wronged; no one would deny that.
He should pay. Justice demanded it. I even re-
sented the fact that he had support and acceptance
from other Christian men.

Then one morning I got a phone call from a
woman in the church who was supporting me.
She said she had been reading in Second Corinthians that morning and had been struck by a passage on forgiveness. For some reason, she thought
I might need to read it.

In this very interesting and powerful passage,
Paul talks about a person who has caused sorrow
in the church at Corinth. Then he instructs them
on how to deal with the offender:

The punishment inflicted on him by the majority is sufficient for him. Now instead, you ought to forgive and comfort him, so that he will not be overwhelmed by excessive sorrow. I urge you, therefore, to reaffirm your love for him. The reason I wrote you was to see if you would stand the test and be obedient in everything. If you forgive anyone, I also forgive him. And what I have forgiven—if there was anything to forgive—I have forgiven in the sight of Christ for your sake, in order that Satan might not outwit us. For we are not unaware of his schemes. (2 Corinthians 2:6-11)

The principle here is pretty straightforward. Don't rub it in, for both your sakes. Not only can the offender be overwhelmed by sorrow (part of that destructive addiction cycle), but also we give Satan the advantage over us by not forgiving.

I was especially struck by Paul's desire that they not just forgive, but that they actually comfort the one who has sinned. What an incredible statement! So different from the popular notion we hear in our culture, that we should focus on and take care of our own needs, our own selves.

I was definitely giving Satan the advantage in my heart and feeling very justified in my sin. I was totally focused on me, until a word of warning came from a friend of mine—*Don't give Satan the advantage*. I knew I needed to get it out and get it over with. That's what we all need.

There were times when I was hurt and Paul did not ask for forgiveness. In many situations, the offending partner never asks for forgiveness. Can we forgive someone who doesn't ask for our forgiveness? Should we forgive that person? I'm afraid the answer is "yes" again. Not forgiving separates us from Christ and takes a physical and emotional toll on us. We cannot afford not to forgive.

For a long time, every new instance brings back all of the old instances, as real and as painful as when they first happened. Brick on brick, I am stuck behind walls of unforgiveness. Each new instance a new brick in an old wall. These protective walls sheltering a core of bitter hatred, keep him out, keep me in. To forgive is to walk back through all the walls until I'm free. I wonder if I can find my way back.

Journal Entry

Paul Talks . . .

To help our business, we made a major move out of state, away from all our family, friends and support. This was a terrifying move for Kathi and a free fall for me. Neither of us had an intact support system and it took us a year to find a new church home.

I was able to avoid pornography for a time, but then I returned like a dog to his vomit and Kathi caught me. God has answered one of my prayers concerning this issue. I've prayed many times that God would give Kathi a discerning spirit and that He would reveal my straying to her. He has done this on several occasions.

The Bible says, "[Y]ou may be sure that your sin will find you out" (Numbers 32:23). And in my case it was almost immediate. The incident involved my taping two videos and taking them with us on a business trip in our motor home.

While Kathi was out doing some shopping I turned on the TV and started one of the videos. As I mentioned, God doesn't give me much rope any longer. Kathi came back unexpectedly. She knew something was wrong when she noticed the TV was on and a tape was in the VCR. We had a terrible breakdown and Kathi threatened to leave me again.

We both felt defeated after this VCR incident. I told Kathi I would do anything to change, but that I had my doubts anything would work. I was close to giving up. This left Kathi with no comfort and little hope for our marriage.

Shortly before this incident, we began attending a church and made some friends. When we got home from our trip, I sought out a man of God, as I had promised. In my mind he was my last hope, and I know God led me to him. It turns out that this man was also a counselor in the church and that he and his wife had a ministry already in place to deal with couples like us. God is in control and does direct our paths.

I met with him and confessed. I told him I felt defeated and I didn't believe Kathi should stay with me any longer. I said I was tired of hurting her and it would probably be best if our marriage ended. I told him I didn't have any hope, I doubted God would forgive me. I even doubted my own salvation.

Through memorized verses and his biblical knowledge, he led me through an understanding of God's desire to forgive and His ability to bring healing and wholeness. This man of God showed me that my willingness to admit defeat was exactly what God needed to begin the healing process. He used Scripture to assure me God wasn't finished with me but the opposite was in fact the truth. He told me I was a child of the King and that God sees me as perfect in His sight—clean, whole, healthy—as the bride of Christ.

All these things I knew, but somehow I had lost their truth in my experience. I had allowed myself to believe a lie and become defeated. He told me to keep short accounts with God and to pray that God would quicken my heart and mind to errors in thought and deed; to live moment by moment.

I allowed myself to experience God's forgiveness. This brought me renewed hope.

I met with him twice a week for a period of two months and then once a month thereafter for another two months. I also became accountable with two other men in the church and attended a weekly men's accountability group. These men prayed with me and for me as God led them. They also called on the phone once a week to check up on me. I told them how often my thoughts wandered off in undesirable directions and of my progress. I still communicate with the counselor on a monthly basis.

Go Ahead and
Meet My Needs

*Realistic and Unrealistic
Expectations*

Each day we are together is a victory. Each day we are together is a guessing game. Each day we are together, we both live with the knowledge that this could be the day of defeat. This could be the day of giving in again. This day is a struggle for him, for me. I can feel his tension. The tension of the struggle. He can feel my tension. The tension of fear. We have moments, sometimes hours of forgetting, but it comes back. Passing cars, magazine racks, catalogs that come in the mail. Television ads, television shows, billboards, newspapers, neighbors, the computer. I need this to end. Is there any way out of this?

FINDING THE WAY OUT is a process. There are no maps. Nobody else really knows where you are. Every situation has its own nuances and peculiarities. All couples have their own individual needs that impact their combined struggle. Did I have needs? Should I have needs? Who should meet those needs? Did he have needs? Should I be the one to meet those needs?

The very idea of being "needy" was foreign to me. I had always been the giver, not the taker, or so I thought. My friends confided their needs and problems to me. I rarely confided mine to them.

I liked being able to help other people. I liked keeping things to myself. I actually felt this was one of my strengths; and it was, at least in part. I did not let people see or know me when I was hurting and in need of help. I believed it was a sign of weakness on my part to want someone's assistance. So by keeping it in, I kept other people out.

To some extent, this included my husband. I was certainly able to verbalize some of my needs to him, but there were many areas I kept him out of because of my lack of trust.

My husband had met many of his own needs through the use of pornography. The addiction had provided an outlet for his tension, his low self-esteem, his anxiety and stress. Changing the pattern was hard for both of us.

We each had needs that were not being fulfilled by the other. It was essential that we name our expectations. We felt it would be good to take a look at our needs, decide if they were being met and develop ways to improve. To this end, we made lists.

Some of my needs were:

- To feel understood
- To trust his commitment to change
- To be informed about how he was doing
- To have him support my need to know

Some of his needs were:

- To trust my commitment to stay in the marriage
- To have freedom from my control
- To feel my support in his struggle

We wrote these down and started to work on them. There were times when we did pretty well and other times when we didn't. I could often see signs of his commitment to change and he could see my commitment to stay in the marriage. But we struggled mightily over my need to be informed and his ability to be sensitive and supportive of that need. And we struggled greatly with my need for control and his need for freedom. We also wrestled with his need for my support and

my desire to see him support himself. A typical
scenario for us might go something like this:

He decides to go fishing, alone.

I have mixed emotions. I really want him to go,
because we need time apart. I am afraid because
he has all that time alone. I think about going with
him, but decide not to, because I really know he
needs to get away and I want to trust him.

He goes fishing. He has a good time and I have
a good time. We need this time apart.

As the time approaches for him to come home,
my mind begins the guessing game of how he did.
I pray about it. I know this is not my battle, not
my place to second-guess his every move. I feel
better knowing the Lord is in control.

He comes home. He launches into stories about
fish, streams and lakes.

I want to know only one thing.

He doesn't mention it.

I get tense. I want him to volunteer how his day
went with temptation.

He doesn't.

I don't want to ask. I do. And when I do, I am
full of tension and anger that I had to ask.

He reacts to my tension and anger. He says, "It
went fine. No problems."

I want details.

He wants peace.

We struggled like this, trying to figure out what
was OK to say, to ask; what was OK to need, to
want.

Through all this turmoil emerged an ever
clearer picture of what was and was not healthy
for each of us. I began to understand that my
husband couldn't meet my every need and
shouldn't be expected to. He began to understand which needs he could and should meet.
This was progress, but there was still something
missing.

Sometimes, I felt hopeless and inadequate and
very much alone. Getting to my core needs wasn't
easy for me. Many of them had nothing to do with
my husband. No matter what he did or didn't do,
he couldn't meet them. These needs were unmet
needs from my childhood. Needs that had to do
with my father being gone; deep feelings of loss
and inadequacy.

One day as I was writing in my journal, this
poem came spilling out on the page.

> A certain kind of song,
>   a certain kind of voice;
> A certain kind of look,
>   a certain kind of choice.
> Certain words bring back that certain feeling,
>   that I certainly thought was dead
>   and most certainly gone.
> I never knew for certain
>   where that certain feeling
>   birthed its uncertain self,
>   but certainly this time, it caught me by
>   surprise.

I was so certain that I would certainly
not see its face, feel its force, again.
This sudden surge of certainty,
that it will always be there,
certainly submerged, certainly covered,
certainly hidden in the shadows,
has certainly surprised me,
made me want to cry,
made me want to lie down in my uncertainty
and certainly die.

Journal Entry

It stopped me short. I knew this poem had to do with old needs, needs I had long before I met Paul. I also knew he could not and should not be expected to meet them. These needs I now take to the Lord. I have found He really is a loving Father, He really is always there. He really does love me no matter what and won't ever leave me. This sounds so simple, but I remember vividly the day I really got it.

I attended a ladies' Bible study periodically. This particular Thursday morning in early December, we had a lesson on, of all things, John 3:16: "For God so loved the world that he gave his one and only Son, that whoever believes in him shall not perish but have eternal life."

I thought, *I've heard this a million times.* But I listened and found the teaching about giving gifts comforting and convicting.

When our leader for that day finished, she asked a question, "What was the true purpose behind God giving His only Son, Jesus?" After a pause, she answered her own query: "To express a love that is inexpressible."

In closing, the class leader asked us to personalize the verse, by putting our own name in it and then writing down what we felt.

I started thinking of someone else and how good this exercise would be for that person, because she really needed to know how much God loved her. Then I stopped short and realized I wasn't doing what the leader had asked at all. I prayed, asking God to help me really know this verse was for me, Kathi.

As I prayed, I saw a huge balloon filling, getting bigger and bigger until there was no limit to its hugeness, no end to its circumference. I felt its immensity in a way I never had. I seemed to be inside it, surrounded by it. I was stunned. I wrote down my thoughts.

This is SO BIG—so massive . . . unimaginable love, indescribable sacrifice. I am purchased with a price—I am worth more than I ever could have known or imagined to the Son of God. It is bigger than I thought it was, too big for comprehension. I am His gift to Himself.

Journal Entry

I sat there stunned and shaken. I couldn't get out of there fast enough. I wanted to be alone. I wanted to savor this incredible experience and think about what it meant.

As I drove home, I knew fully what it was to be loved greatly. My needs shifted to a different place in my heart. What I had wanted so desperately for so long—security and love from a man—was so small next to what I had, this indescribable love of GOD. I really got it, understood it! Then I was able to get a handle on what I really needed from my husband.

Setting Realistic Expectations

Each of us has needs. We are human. We have physical needs, emotional needs, sexual needs. I grew up thinking one great love of my life would come along and fulfill all my needs. I would experience total fulfillment with the man I married and I would meet all of his needs. I would be the very best wife anyone could imagine and he would be the most unbelievably great husband. I thought we would be madly in love and have a wonderful sexual experience together throughout our lives.

Many of the needs I thought my great love would fill cannot be filled by any real person. No other person can be everything I want. No other person is responsible for my happiness.

There were, and still are, some very real needs and expectations in my relationship. Because of my husband's addiction, some of those needs and expectations are different than they might be in a marriage where there is no addiction.

Besides trying to meet each other's physical, emotional and sexual needs, we also were trying to meet some relational needs that came up as a result of our shared problem. We felt it necessary to come to agreement on these issues.

1. What is and is not acceptable behavior. He made definite commitments not to seek out or view any kind of pornography. He wrote this resolution down for both of us to look at when we needed to.

2. What he can and cannot assure me of. He could and did assure me he loved me, that he wanted to be in partnership with me, that he had committed his life to God first and then to me and our family. He assured me he would be honest with me and continue his walk toward integrity. He couldn't assure me he would never fail.

3. What information is healthy for me to ask and for him to give. We came to understand that it was healthier for him to discuss specific struggles in detail with a supportive male, not with me. The dynamic of his telling me, my becoming hurt and angry and his feeling guilty and angry at my response to his confession was incredibly destructive. My need to know every single detail was in itself an unhealthy attempt at control.

We agreed he needed to have someone to be accountable to and that it was best for that person to be another Christian man. We also agreed that it was healthy for him to tell me if he was struggling and for me to tell him if I noticed him slipping. But we agreed we should redirect each other's focus back to God if we saw each other slipping.

Certainly, as married partners, it is our desire to meet as many of the needs of our mates as we can, but we can take responsibility for our own fulfillment in some areas. We have friends, family and outside interests which all play a part in a fulfilled life. I don't believe this lets the other partner off the hook, but it does allow each of us to become stronger, more balanced. We all have a desire to have an intimate relationship with our partners, but there are limits to what they can and cannot do for us and what we should and should not expect from them.

It helped me greatly to put my expectations down on paper. Seeing the lists cleared up some of my own haziness about them. It also helped Paul to read what I expected from him. Here are my lists:

HE CAN	HE CAN'T
Be honest and open.	Bring every thought under my scrutiny.
Commit to no more pornography.	Say he will never fail that commitment.
Be supportive.	Be my only support.
Let me vent my frustrations.	Be my whipping post.
Be loving.	Make me feel loved.
Reassure me.	Make me feel secure.
Be a spiritual leader.	Fill a void that only God can fill.
Desire me sexually.	Make me feel attractive and desirable.

I SHOULD	I SHOULDN'T
Expect a commitment to change.	Expect him to change overnight.
Expect him to grow in strength.	Expect him to be superman in this area.

I found it very difficult to accept these limitations of my expectations, even after I had written them. I wanted Paul to make up for what he had done "to me." It was difficult to honor him and desire him. The truth was, I had stopped allowing him to meet my emotional and sexual needs. I kept him at a distance; I wouldn't allow myself to be vulnerable. I was cut off from him even while saying, "Why won't you think of me? Why are you so selfish?" Deep down, I wasn't about to let him meet my needs. I felt that if I did, I would be vulnerable and he would have the advantage.

I found it very hard to take my eyes off my own needs and realize that he had needs too. As our relationship began to heal—almost as a by-product of our spiritual healing—Paul was able to articulate some of his own needs and I was able to actually hear and support them. Some of his needs were:

- To feel my support.
- To know that I loved him.
- To know that I honored and desired him.
- To know that other men were praying for him.

There were times, and still are, when I had real joy in being able to support him, love him, desire him. There were also times when I had absolutely no energy or desire to give him anything. I felt he would always take care of himself and I shouldn't be expected to try to fulfill his needs.

The culture we live in has a lot to say about getting our own needs met. It is a culture of selfish individualism. There are classes, seminars and weekend retreats teaching the ideals of self-esteem and self-fulfillment. I believe we all need a healthy self-esteem and much of our addictive behavior is born because of a lack in this area. However, I do not believe the answer can be found inside ourselves. I do not believe we will be fulfilled by selfishly trying to get our own needs met. I found when I could get past my own needs and actually see my husband's, I really did have a desire to meet some of them. I also had a desire to pray for him. I wanted him to be happy. I wanted him to be at peace.

The key for me was, and continually is, vulnerability, opening up and letting someone outside myself meet my needs. There can and should be a balance between a healthy need for other people in our lives and an unhealthy dependence on outsiders. There should also be a balance between getting our own needs met and meeting the needs of others.

For a long period of time I felt I was living in a Dr. Seuss book. It went something like this:

Your needs, my needs,
My needs, yours.
All these windows,
All these doors.

My needs, your needs,
Your needs, mine.
Getting needs met,
One at a time.

"You meet my needs."
"No, mine, this time."
Who meets whose needs
To continue the rhyme?

Journal Entry

But not so much anymore. Growing in my relationship with Christ has given me strength and clarity, health and peace. He truly does meet all the needs I'm willing to relinquish. He brings all of life into perspective. Daily, I hold on to this promise: "And my God will meet all your needs according to his glorious riches in Christ Jesus" (Philippians 4:19).

This is a very long process. I wish it wasn't. I get tired of it. To think of this as a whole is too overwhelming. Piece by piece is how I have to do it. What is going on right now? One big victory, one little defeat. One little victory, one big defeat. But always going on. Not quitting. Getting stronger. Going in the right direction. Things are so much better. Each day I feel stronger. Most days I feel sure of our future.

Journal Entry

Paul Talks . . .

My progress can be mapped in direct proportion to my commitment to God and my willingness to follow Him. In my mind, no secular program or counselor can make a permanent change for someone suffering from sexual addiction. Healing is a process for both of us; there is no instant cure.

I believe evil forces exist which only God can battle. My part is to give my life over to Him and admit my inability to win without Him. God is able to finish what He started in me. He sees the battle as already won, and indeed it is. The reality of these truths sounds too simple, yet my struggles remain very real and present. I am free from the bondage of this sin, but not the possibility of failing.

Secrecy is the enemy and denial is his comrade. When I first was confronted with my inability to quit these patterns of addiction, I told Kathi everything about my past and present difficulties and problems. I don't recommend this now that we've gone through it together.

I do believe a man must become blatantly honest with someone to whom he can be accountable, but his wife should not take the place of God in being able to hear all and forgive all. She is not his confessional. This unburdening of his guilt should be to God and to another man, or men, who can support him, correct him and direct him.

I have found such men within the church body. I can tell them honestly where I am and what needs I have and

*they support me. I find the dynamics very interesting.
When I am being honest and seeking accountability, my
desire to stray and my temptations are greatly diminished. The problem is out in the open. Without secrecy
and denial, God's power over the enemy is more readily
demonstrated.*

Rebuilding the Dream Team

Living with What's Real

We are so different, he and I. The differences are in perspective, not appearance. The days and years we have been together, it is the differences that have made the difference. The closeness of our situations magnified the distance between us. The closer we became, the more the differences mattered. It seemed impossible for him to change his perspective, equally impossible for me to change mine. But somehow we have remained friends in the midst of it. We have built some bridges. The distance between us is diminishing and the differences are not so big.

IN WRITING THIS BOOK, my life is exposed to you in a way that I would never have chosen. In the beginning, it was a stretch for me to even discuss this area of my life with a counselor in a closed room where no one else could hear or know. Even now, I can count on one hand the people with whom I talk openly about this area of struggle.

This book is a product of God's working in my life. I have not been a quick learner. The freedom that is mine in Christ was left dormant, unapplied to this area of my life for years.

I struggled.

We struggled.

We lost.

Finally, I quit.

Gave up.

Lost hope.

Then and only then, did I say, "OK, Lord, I can't do this. I don't have any more reserves. I'm done.

"Take it.

"TAKE IT.

"*TAKE IT!*"

And then later: "What is it I'm supposed to learn from this? I'm ready to learn it and get on with my life. The passion that has preoccupied my mind all these years has worn itself out. I'm exhausted from this fight. I CAN'T WIN."

When I picked up God's Word, in wonder took it in and applied it to this struggle, the "peace that passes all understanding," filled me with "the incredible riches that are in Christ Jesus." All I ever needed. All I could ever need. Answers to every question. And so . . . to live.

Rebuilding couldn't begin without God. I was in a holding pattern, trying desperately to hold it all together. My arms were too full to do any work on the building. I kept thinking, *Give it up.* These words sound so simple. They are not. I broke it down into manageable pieces.

GIVE

To present voluntarily and, without expecting compensation,
to place in someone's care.

IT

The addiction;
the obsession with the addiction;
control.

UP

to God.

What Is Real?

Paul and I share a problem that impacts our lives. We have been living with this problem for many years, this shared problem that will not go away. But this dilemma is not the sum total of our relationship. We are together because we love each other, because we are friends, because we share a commitment to stay together until we die.

There is much more to our lives than this one thing that threatens our union. We have decided, with God's help, that we will not let it impact every part of our existence as a couple.

As we examined our lives, we discovered other things that are real for us. These might not be real for you. Your relationship might not be salvageable because of ongoing sin on the part of your partner. Not everything can be fixed. Not every relationship can be put back together. But for us, these things are true.

1. Our standing in Christ. We are both Christians. We are both growing and maturing in our walk with the Lord. In Christ, we are free. The apostle Paul wrote:

> Therefore, there is now no condemnation for those who are in Christ Jesus, because through Christ Jesus the law of

the Spirit of life set me free from the law
of sin and death. (Romans 8:1-2)

What a glorious place to be. God has promised to
forgive and forget our sins when we repent of them.

I, even I, am he who blots out your trans-
gressions, for my own sake, and remem-
bers your sins no more. (Isaiah 43:25)

If we confess our sins, he is faithful and
just and will forgive us our sins and purify
us from all unrighteousness. (1 John 1:9)

2. *The promises of God.* The Bible is full of promises
of abundant life in Christ. These promises are real.
God doesn't break His word. People do. I do; you
do; we do. But God doesn't. It helped me to put my
very own name in these verses. The more personal-
ized they are for me, the more I can own them.

For his anger lasts only a moment,
    but his favor lasts a lifetime;
weeping may remain for a night,
    but rejoicing comes in the morning.
                                    (Psalm 30:5)

The LORD is close to the brokenhearted
    and saves those who are crushed in
        spirit. (34:18)

Though I walk in the midst of trouble,
    you preserve my life;

> you stretch out your hand against the
>   anger of my foes,
>   with your right hand you save me.
> The LORD will fulfill his purpose for
>   me;
>   your love, O LORD, endures for-
>   ever—
>   do not abandon the works of your
>   hands. (138:7-8)

The thief comes only to steal and kill and destroy; I have come that they may have life, and have it to the full. (John 10:10)

And we know that in all things God works for the good of those who love him, who have been called according to his purpose. (Romans 8:28)

He who did not spare his own Son, but gave him up for us all—how will he not also, along with him, graciously give us all things? (8:32)

And on and on and on. God's Word is full of promises. The more we fill our minds with His promises, the more we find ourselves trusting Him.

3. The need for reconciliation. After betrayal and forgiveness comes reconciliation. If you have been cut off from your partner through betrayal, anger and bitterness, how do you restore your relationship? You can't go back and have what you once had, but you can move forward together seeking a new, stronger relationship that works for both of you.

The word *reconcile* means to become friendly or peaceable again, to restore, to bring into agreement or harmony. It takes a concentrated effort to bring a relationship back into harmony. It doesn't just automatically happen because you both want it to. Old patterns have to be unlearned and replaced with new ways of interacting.

4. An understanding of addiction. There are always reasons for addiction. My husband and his counselor explored these reasons during counseling sessions at which I was not present. It helped me to be told what some of these reasons were.

- *The family dynamic.* There are usually unhealthy family dynamics in an addict's background. My husband felt very lonely as a child, even though he was one of five children. He experienced his parents as distant and non-nurturing. Much of the time, he felt isolated, with low self-esteem.

- *Early introduction to pornography.* There has almost always been an early experience with some kind of pornography in an addict's background. My husband began looking at erotic magazines very early in adolescence and developed a pattern of masturbation before he was in high school. This impacted his ability to relate to girls in a healthy, nonsexual way. He became more introverted. During his teens, he visited a prostitute and found that experience very unsatisfying. He preferred fantasy to reality.

- *The dynamics of addiction.* Feelings of stress, shame, low self-esteem are common among addicts. Sexual stimulation is often used to soothe those feelings. Then come intense guilt and self-loathing. Together—the thrilling highs, the secrecy, the crushing guilt, the self-loathing—they become an addictive cycle. As with any addiction, the sexual addict needs more and more stimulation to produce the desired high. The pit is deep; for some, there is no bottom.

5. *Help from reading books on the subject.* We found that being more educated on the subject of addiction helped us recognize patterns and deal constructively with them. Several excellent books on sexual addiction are available. Some are listed at the end of this chapter.

6. *The importance of communication.* To reconcile, you must talk to each other openly, without shame. I am always amazed by the lack of straightforward communication between married partners. Silence and innuendo have no place in your rebuilding mode. It is unhealthy for him and it is unhealthy for you. Get it out on the table. Develop ground rules for communicating with each

other and then do it. Some great books on communication for couples are available.

I tend to rant and rave when I am hurt and angry. Paul tends to close down and distance himself. I have learned to be a little less talkative and explosive, and Paul has learned to be more forthright and open.

7. *The Lord can redeem our failures.* To "redeem" means to buy or pay off; clear by payment; to buy back. No matter what you have done, no matter what your partner has done, God can and will redeem those failures. He can bring joy out of your worst nightmare. He can take the things that you have damaged and ruined and make them new and whole. I know He can. He has for me.

Way back on that first morning after I found out, I didn't think any good could ever come out of the pain I felt. There appeared to be no way out of the nightmare. But over the years, I have stood by and watched in wonder as God has worked in our lives. He has brought our relationship to a strong, new place. It is not perfect. We are not perfect. But we are not so bogged down with the past, not so stuck in despair when we fail.

The Process of Reconciliation

Reconciling was a process for us, as this whole experience has been. We did not just sit down and say, "OK, let's reconcile and get back together. You do this and I'll do that and then we'll be done." Some of the things we did and said were pretty low and mean. Some things were more noble and useful. We did find that it worked to have a plan. We found ourselves shooting from the hip a little less.

Here are some ideas that might help in rebuilding your relationship. They are not a quick, easy formula. If there is one, we haven't found it. You might do some of these, all of these or none of these. How you rebuild is not as important as choosing to try. We are still working at it.

Step 1: Develop a Plan Together

a. Try to come to an agreement on what is and is not acceptable. We've talked about this in previous chapters, but I want to stress the importance of writing it down. Sometimes we talk and don't write. Then one of us forgets or thinks we heard it differently, and off we go on a round of accusation and misunderstanding.

"You said you wouldn't do this."

"No, I didn't. We decided to do it this way."

"We did? I don't remember that."

We found if we could actually come to an agreement, then it was safer to get it down on paper.

One other thing—it works well to hold your standards up to the Scriptures. The Bible is an excellent resource for developing acceptable boundaries.

b. Try to set realistic goals for your relationship.
Don't set yourselves up for failure. Rebuilding
your relationship is a process. You don't wake up
one morning with a perfect one.

It is better to go slowly in your expectations of
change. I found myself setting pretty high standards for my husband, but significantly lower ones
for myself. I could justify my extreme response to
any failure on his part, no matter how small. I expected him to understand, because, after all, he was
the reason we were doing all this rebuilding.

It took me a while to begin to expect more out
of myself. Interestingly, as I have done that, I have
been able to ease up a bit on my expectations of
Paul. Relationships are not built nor rebuilt in a
day. Accept up front that you are going to suffer
some setbacks. We have suffered many, but we
are progressing.

c. Develop support systems and accountability. You
both need support. You also both need to be accountable. My husband has three men who support him by
praying for him and holding him accountable.

I lagged behind a bit in finding support for myself. I actually didn't think I needed to have someone designated to support me. After all, *he* had the
addiction. But I was wrong. I needed it as much as
he did. Today I have one person with whom I can
be totally honest. This person prays for me and
supports our relationship. I have another person
whom I talk to less frequently, but who is also
there for me when I need her.

There are also support groups for addicts and their spouses. These groups use the twelve-step program and are very helpful for some. What ever you do, don't go it alone. You'll never make it. Silence kills. You need other people, and believe it or not, they need you.

d. Begin rebuilding intimacy. To be vulnerable means you are capable of, or susceptible to, being wounded or hurt. Intimacy requires trust and vulnerability.

How vulnerable should you allow yourself to be? What does intimacy look like? Transparency, sharing, closeness and acceptance are all parts of vulnerability in a relationship.

Who should initiate these? I believe you both should. I also believe you should honor each other and protect each other's vulnerabilities. I have to be careful not to use things Paul has shared with me against him at a later date. When you are transparent and share deep feelings, you need to be sensitive to each other. Many times a hasty word can cut off the one who is attempting to reach out.

It is risky to be vulnerable. Take it slow. Little risks, then bigger ones. Accept each other and support each other. In time, you will slowly become closer and more open in your relationship.

e. Try making your home a stronghold. The apostle Paul admonishes us in this area: "Rather, clothe yourselves with the Lord Jesus Christ, and do not think about how to gratify the desires of the sinful

nature" (Romans 13:14). For us that meant ending
our evening TV viewing. It meant putting the computer in a room that is not off by itself. It meant
buying a program for our computer that limits what
can be viewed. It meant limiting what comes into
our home in the form of magazines and newspapers.

We decided together that we wanted our home
to be a place of strength and safety for both of us.
There is enough temptation outside the home that
we have to deal with; we don't need to bring it inside. We live in a society obsessed and saturated
with sex. There is no way to escape the images
completely. Making our home a safe place has
helped us both become stronger.

The Bible is clear in its teaching on this matter:

> Test everything. Hold on to the good.
> Avoid every kind of evil. (1 Thessalonians
> 5:21-22)

> Submit yourselves, then, to God. Resist the
> devil, and he will flee from you. (James 4:7)

You might not want to give up some of the
things that will help him grow stronger. He might
not want to give up some of the things you feel
would be helpful. Whatever you decide, you both
need to come to an agreement on what to keep,
what not to keep. It takes some forbearance, but it
has helped us to keep our home a place of
strength.

Step 2: Develop and Use Good Tools

We have found a number of good tools that have worked for us in rebuilding. Perhaps they will be helpful to you as well.

a. Visualization. One of the things that has been very helpful for Paul is visualization. He pictures Jesus being right next to him or holding on to his hand.

Our minds are mine fields. Much of our time is spent merely thinking random thoughts. It is good to guard your mind. I find it helpful to stop myself when bad thoughts come and pray. I visualize taking the thought in my hands and dropping it into God's.

I also visualize our marriage working. I always used to see it falling apart. It helps immensely to hold in my mind a picture of us together.

b. Confess and fill—breathe out, breathe in. Confessing our sins when they happen and asking God to fill us with His Spirit can be very powerful tools in breaking addictive cycles. It is also a powerful way to live.

Some people use the phrase "breathe out, breathe in" to describe a similar process. Breathe out sin, breathe in forgiveness. The key to using this tool is to use it right away. Don't harbor bad thoughts; don't let sin pitch its tent in your heart. Get rid of it.

c. Assurances. It is important to give each other assurances, especially as you start to rebuild your relationship. Assure each other of your love. Assure each other you are committed to keeping your mutual promises.

Develop some new ways to speak about an old problem. Your conversation is powerful. The words you use with each other have great impact. It is important to stay away from phrases that you have both gotten used to using, phrases that tear down.

We found we were each using words that felt defeating to the other person. Sometimes when we discussed Paul's use of pornography, he said, "I will do it again, I know I will." Even though I knew he couldn't promise me he would never go back, this statement devastated me. He feels he cannot trust himself and without God's help, he will fall. I understand that, but I can't stand to hear him say it in those words.

Several times, during discussions, I have said, "If this happens again, I will divorce you." This statement devastates Paul. He feels powerless and angry when he hears it. We agreed to stay away from these two phrases and others also.

It might be good to develop a list of phrases you both hate and then stay away from them. It is also good to affirm each other, to tell your partner you are proud of him, to commend your mate for the growth you see.

d. Pray together daily. There is absolutely no substitute for prayer in our lives. In my early years as a Christian, I thought prayer was something you had to do, something you should do. However, I never could do it consistently.

As I have matured, I realized prayer is an incredible gift. It's such fun. Talking to God. Taking all my problems, big and little, to Him and discussing them. It is like having your own personal therapist on call at all times, only better.

I have seen God answer many prayers! As I see answers, I am prompted to pray more. The more I pray, the more answers I see. What a great circle to be in.

It has been a wonderful, growing source of strength for my husband and me to pray together. Our schedule is flexible, so we usually do so in the morning and again at bedtime. I realize this does not work for everyone. Many days and nights when one of us has been discouraged with the progress of our relationship, the other's prayer has been a solid rock to hang on to.

We have learned so much about each other by praying together. For instance, I know my husband wants to be a good father and a good husband. I hear him pray it every day. If you can't pray together every day, you might set a goal to pray at least once a week together. We have found relationship building is much easier when we pray together regularly.

e. Read the Bible together daily. How can we know the promises we have in Christ if we don't read His Word? How can we know if He has anything

to say about our situation? How can we know if
He cares about us if we don't ever open up His
book and see for ourselves?

Paul and I have a time each morning when we
read together. We usually do not read out loud
and we each read in a different place in the Scriptures, but we are together. We usually discuss
something that stands out for one of us that day.
God's Word is so powerful it convicts and cuts to
the heart in a way our individual words cannot.
The writer of Hebrews says:

> For the word of God is living and active.
> Sharper than any double-edged sword, it
> penetrates even to dividing soul and spirit,
> joints and marrow; it judges the thoughts
> and attitudes of the heart. (Hebrews 4:12)

I feel closer to Paul when I hear him talking
about the Scripture he is reading. I feel like I
know him better. He knows me better. The Word
of God has answers for our problems. We won't
find them if we don't read them.

f. Encouragement. It is good to say nice things to
each other, to encourage each other. This sounds
so simple, so easy, but I don't always find it to be
that way. I don't know why nice things don't just
roll off my tongue, but they don't.

In order to rebuild our broken relationship,
Paul and I need to point out the good we see. We
can say things like:

"I have confidence in you."

"I know you can do this."

"I see you trying hard."

"I see how well you're doing."

Discouragement comes along without a lot of help from anyone. Encouraging each other to do better and to keep trying when we fail spurs us on to success.

Step 3: Develop Healthy Lives

Being healthy and maintaining health are things we must work at. There are a number of ways to succeed in this area.

a. Develop individual and shared interests. Addictions steal a lot of time. When you are in the process of breaking free, you need to fill the void that now exists. This is where outside interests and hobbies play an important role.

You can do a multitude of things, some together and some individually. Here are a few to get you thinking: reading, writing poetry, painting, ceramics, gardening, learning to play the piano, fishing, hunting, an exercise program. My husband developed his interest in fly-fishing. I love to garden. We like to read together.

Look outward together and find ways you can minister to others. You can get involved in many organizations that are already in place, so you don't have to start from scratch. Your church is a good place to look. If possible find a way to minister to others together.

People all around you have needs. It is a healthy exercise to focus on someone else's needs for a while. This keeps you from becoming short-sighted and introverted, especially when you have addiction in your family. Your ability to minister to others can be shut down by addiction.

One unhealthy thought I have now and then is, *If we get too close to people they might find out*. Paul and I both have felt ashamed and inadequate, as if we have nothing to give to others. As we discussed this, we wondered if this is not a favorite lie Satan uses to keep us ineffective. We can and should go outside ourselves. We don't have to live out our lives behind closed doors. As we take the focus off the addiction and put it on others, we find that suddenly we have time for life!

b. Keep your mind healthy. Think good thoughts. Don't entertain the lies of Satan. He will attack both of you as you move through the healing process. Be on your guard against him. He is a liar.

Here are some of the lies he whispers in my ear about Paul:

"He doesn't love you."

"He doesn't think you're desirable."

"He wants a big-busted blonde."

"He is with you because it's easy and convenient."

"He is lying to you."

"It's all another elaborate scheming lie."

"He thinks he could do better."

"He needs pornography because you are not
    enough."

"You'll never be what he wants."

"You'll never be enough."

If I don't take my thoughts captive, I end up in trouble. I start thinking and imagining and pretty soon I develop a whole scenario in my head. Interestingly, these scenarios are almost always bad, hurtful things. David writes:

> O LORD, you have searched me
>   and you know me.
> You know when I sit and when I rise;
>   you perceive my thoughts from afar.
> You discern my going out
>   and my lying down;
>   you are familiar with all my ways.
> Before a word is on my tongue
>   you know it completely, O LORD.
>   (Psalm 139:1-4)

A little scary, isn't it? Or maybe incredibly comforting. God knows every single thought that pops into your mind. He is intimately acquainted with all your ways. It is both wonderful and heart-stopping to be known so intimately.

I have discovered I can control my thoughts, and this is what God expects of me. The apostle

Paul writes in Second Corinthians: "We demolish arguments and every pretension that sets itself up against the knowledge of God, and we take captive every thought to make it obedient to Christ" (10:5).

A huge part of my husband's addiction was in his thoughts. A big part of my obsession with his addiction was in my thoughts. We both have had to work hard on controlling what goes on in our minds.

Not long ago, my husband said to me, "Stop trying to read my mind!"

I had been anticipating his thoughts and actually felt I could tell what he was thinking. He didn't appreciate it. It was not a healthy pastime for me either.

I wrote in my journal:

I really want to help. I have a desire to see him have victory and feel confidence in himself, but I don't always say and do what I would like. I find myself having new thoughts of his betrayal when we go through any kind of stress or trauma. I think I know his thoughts before he thinks them. I don't.

Journal Entry

c. *Don't just "act natural."* Our normal, natural reactions do not always promote rebuilding, at least, not in our relationship. My natural response to hurt is pain, anger and retaliation. "You did that to me, so here, take this!"

Another step in the rebuilding process is to begin controlling your natural urges. To mature. Romans 12 is an incredible passage of Scripture. It is long, so I will just give you some excerpts, but it helped me to read it all every day for a while. I let it sink in, way in, where it could make a difference.

> Love must be sincere. Hate what is evil; cling to what is good. Be devoted to one another in brotherly love. Honor one an-other above yourselves. . . . Be joyful in hope, patient in affliction, faithful in prayer. . . .
> Bless those who persecute you; bless and do not curse. . . .
> Do not repay anyone evil for evil. . . . If it is possible, as far as it depends on you, live at peace with everyone. Do not take re-venge, my friends, but leave room for God's wrath. . . . Do not be overcome by evil, but overcome evil with good. (12:9-21)

Can you believe it? I think God must have looked down through the centuries and known I would be in a place of despair, hurt and anger and He decided to send me a message about how to cope. Everything looks different when I look up from reading these verses. I know that it is possi-ble to control my reactions. I might not want to, but I can.

Recently, I jotted down a few of my natural re-actions along with a few possible responses:

Natural Reaction	*Godly Response*
Hurt.	Acknowledge that you are hurting.
Anger.	Look at him. What is he feeling?
	Defeat, anger, self-loathing?
	Ask God to use your anger for good.
Bitterness.	Take action to forgive.
	Don't hold hurt.

And then this prayer came to me, when I was feeling defeated with my natural reactions to perceived threats:

Dear Lord,

Will I always be reacting? Reacting to some perceived wrong? Reacting to my circumstances? Will I never be pro-active? Taking the initiative for good? Teach me to calm myself in You. Teach me to rest and not react.

Today, I began by reacting to a perceived tension. Then it escalated into reacting to perceived wrongs. Then off I went in my mind down the path of thoughts and reactions.

I know this path. I've been here before. This path leads to enslavement. Please teach me not to fear . . . or at least to face my fear, use Your strength and stare it down. Help me to remember that You are my steady rock. I don't need to react.

Journal Prayer

d. Grasp your own fallibility. It is healthy to know your own weaknesses, to know you can fail. At the same time, you must not wallow in your frailties, just simply be aware of them.

In our relationship, the focus was on my husband's failures for a very long time. We both knew how weak he could be in the area of sexual addiction.

However, as he began to heal and become stronger, some of my weaknesses began to surface—my need for control, my desire to punish him for hurting me, my feelings of hatred. I was not the long-suffering angel I had envisioned. As a matter of fact, I could be as mean and selfish as anybody.

We both have areas of weakness. Mine are not necessarily nicer weaknesses than his. We are both prone to sin. We both need to leave room for failure in ourselves and in each other. A great passage of Scripture in Romans is applicable to this situation:

> I know that nothing good lives in me, that is, in my sinful nature. For I have the desire to do what is good, but I cannot carry it out. For what I do is not the good I want to do; no, the evil I do not want to do—this I keep on doing. . . .
>
> What a wretched man I am! Who will rescue me from this body of death? Thanks be to God—through Jesus Christ our Lord! (Romans 7:18-19, 24-25)

It starts out looking pretty dark, but it ends on a glorious note. It's good to remember through the rebuilding process that we are both fallible. We need each other's help.

e. Take note and celebrate. It is very important to notice the victories and celebrate them. We have had many in the last couple of years. Some were major victories in big battles; some were little, hardly noticeable ones. But big or small, we have found it is discouraging for both of us when the other person doesn't acknowledge progress.

I especially have had to work on this. With the great emotional distance we had to go, I felt if I reacted too exuberantly to my husband's progress, he might stop where he was and then slip back. On occasion, I purposely minimized some of the victories, thinking, *Yes, he did that, but what about this?*

In the end, I found my attitude did the very thing I didn't want it to do: It made him think, *What's the use? She never sees any progress. Why should I try so hard?*

There were also times when I thought I was making progress, and he was the one who didn't see or acknowledge it. I wanted him to verbally recognize that I was doing better.

Acknowledgment and affirmation are extremely important parts of rebuilding a relationship. Try to find some progress and reward it with a good word or a little written note. From time to time have a real celebration: Go out to dinner or get away for a weekend together and focus on how far you have come and where you want to go together. Celebrate your progress and keep going!

f. See each other through God's eyes. When my husband was challenged by a Christian counselor to see himself as God sees him, he was finally able to break out of his cycle of addiction. He is not a bad person, unworthy, shameful and vile because he has this particular sin. He is a saint, redeemed, a child of the family. Grasping that he is a saint who sometimes sins, not a sinner constantly failing at trying to be good, was enlightening. We are not trying to be worthy; in Christ, we are worthy.

It is important to make a concrete decision to give this addiction to God, wholly, completely, holding nothing back. My husband gave up many things during our marriage, but he could not give up this addiction for any long period of time. When he began to see he was in a spiritual battle, he used God's Word to have victory.

I, too, had to totally surrender myself and my husband to God. I had to give up taking on the "God" role in his life. It was healthy for me to let the Lord deal with him.

What a relief! Seeing ourselves and each other through God's eyes clears up a lot of confusion.

g. Live in hope. Living without hope is a miserable existence. I have lived both ways. I have had periods of optimism, filled with hope for our marriage, and I have had periods of despair, feeling things were hopeless.

What I know today is that Paul and I have hope. It is by no means over, but there is hope. We are together. We are rebuilding. We have come through the fire. You can, too. The foundation, the rock on which our hope stands, is Jesus Christ. Without Him we would most certainly be miserable. Apart from Him, we would most certainly be divorced.

The apostle Paul writes, "And hope does not disappoint us, because God has poured out his love into our hearts by the Holy Spirit, whom he has given us" (Romans 5:5). There is hope, for you, for your partner, for your marriage. I want to encourage you to hang on to hope.

I'm staying because I choose to, knowing it might not work. I'm giving a chance to our union, acknowledging the pain in my chest. Caring enough for this person to do whatever it takes. Fully aware that it might not make any difference, and I might just be delaying the end. Staying while there's an outside chance that healing can take place and hope be restored to its rightful place on the shelf next to love.

Journal Entry

Paul Talks . . .

We have been married eleven years now and my Christian walk grows continually. We pray together and read our Bibles during breakfast. And we pray together as we go to sleep each night.

We have moved again, since Kathi first started the writing of this book, close to our grandchildren and families once more. God orchestrated this move and we found a wonderful church right away.

He has also led me to a couple of wonderful brothers in the body to be accountable to. We meet for lunch once a week and I keep a journal as well. Kathi and I are also part of a weekly growth group and are making plans to open our house for this purpose.

When relatives and people who know us view our marriage they see a well-matched, in-love couple, not two people struggling with any major issues and definitely not a marriage in jeopardy. On the outside we have the perfect marriage. We are a fun-loving couple. People look up to us as an example of a good marriage. We get along and have a good time together.

We are a happy couple for the most part. We are best friends and have a good sex life. We would agree that our marriage is strong in most areas and that we are happy with each other. Neither of us would want anything to happen to our marriage.

We are deeply in love with each other and strongly attached to each other's families as well. But bad things happen in good marriages and sin can destroy that which is otherwise great.

Healing for me began when I determined I needed help for myself, not for Kathi. I needed to admit my inability to make myself well. I had to let God take control of my healing.

A significant portion of Kathi's healing took place during the writing of this book. We have both found that writing things out in detail is a healthy, healing exercise.

I have found many Scriptures that have helped me through my healing journey. Here are a few which speak to the issues I have dealt with.

> How precious to me are your thoughts,
> O God!
> How vast is the sum of them!
> Were I to count them,
> they would outnumber the grains of
> sand.
> When I awake,
> I am still with you.
> (Psalm 139:17-18)

> Avoid it, do not travel on it;
> turn from it and go on your way.
> (Proverbs 4:15)

For these commands are a lamp,
　　this teaching is a light,
and the corrections of discipline
　　are the way to life,
keeping you from the immoral woman,
　　from the smooth tongue of the wayward
　　　　wife.
Do not lust in your heart after her
　　　　　beauty
　　or let her captivate you with her eyes.
　　　　　　　　(6:23-25)

My son, give me your heart
　　and let your eyes keep to my ways.
　　　　　　　　　　(23:26)

As iron sharpens iron,
　　so one man sharpens another. . . .
As water reflects a face,
　　so a man's heart reflects the man.
　　　　　　　　　　(27:17, 19)

EPILOGUE

As Paul and I look back over recent years, we are blessed by the evidence of God working in each of our lives. When we met, we were both "walking wounded," and both of us had wandered away from God. Neither one had the internal resources to change.

When we, individually, made decisions to repent and return to the Lord, we were optimistic about God's ability to change our marriage. But it wasn't smooth sailing. We had to deal with the effects of sin in our lives. Errors plagued our thinking and we both had old habits to deal with.

Although Paul and I had each given our lives to Christ many years previously, we turned our backs on what we knew was right. Consequently, we lost whatever spiritual maturity we had once gained. Our regrowth was slow, as you have seen in reading this book.

One thing was in our favor, however. We both believed in the sanctity of marriage. We had strong convictions that divorce was only an option for a Christian in the case of adultery (Matthew 19:1-9) and even then, it was not the only option. Despite this, the thought of divorce often resurfaced, particularly with me, when we despaired

129

over some relational impasse. In these moments of weakness, running away seemed like an easier approach than weathering the storm. Still it was our total commitment to our marriage that always steadied us and restored sanity in the end.

We believe marriage is ordained by God, it is a binding contract, a covenant relationship. The devastating thing about sexual sin is that it breaks this covenant. However, even in the case of adultery, marriages can be restored. Divorce is not the only option and it is certainly not the desired option, despite the alarming number of church couples who go that route. Divorce doesn't solve the problems, it aggravates them, leaving individuals to struggle alone against sinful passions, a sense of betrayal and anger. Dissolving the marriage stymies restoration. Though it offers a temporary release from pain, it further postpones the possibility of healing. It becomes a hindrance, not a help.

Though we shared frankly about our struggles and foolishness during moments of weakness, we want to restate with total sincerity: We are fully committed to God's plan for marriage. He wants the best for us and so do we.

Some may say that is well and good, but they want to know how we are today. What's the state of our relationship? Are things any better than they were? How are we faring on a day-to-day basis? And they have a right to ask since we took the initiative to open up our lives in the first place. Here is our frank assessment of the state of our union.

We are first and foremost committed to our walk with Christ and our relationship with each other. However, we still have issues we are dealing with, we still have areas of weakness. As we gain victory in one area of sin, we gain insight into new areas that need repentance and change.

When Paul and I talk about commitment, we mean we are willing to work on our marriage. Here are some of our goals as they relate to the issues we are currently working on.

Paul's Commitments

- To tell the truth; be open, honest and forthright with any problems I have with my commitments.
- To avoid sexual arousal to any stimulus other than my wife.
- To avoid any sexually suggestive pictures or articles, including those on television and the internet.
- To stay out of video stores when alone.
- To avoid flirtations and sexualizing women in my mind and with my eyes.
- To be open and honest with my accountability partners concerning these matters.
- To keep my sexual thoughts only on my wife.
- To alter my viewing area when distracted by another woman.
- In all these areas, I am fully committed to God, my wife and my marriage.

Kathi's Commitments

- To grow in my dependence on God for Paul's healing.
- To stay out of the role of policewoman.
- To stay in our marriage.
- To continue my own healing process.

It is the power of Christ working in us that has brought about marital restoration. Only as He enables us will we be able to keep these commitments.

We have been open and honest about some very private aspects of our lives. The telling of our story has been a healing process. It is our hope that being honest about our struggles with sexual sin and its consequences will open the door for God's healing in your marriage as well.

RECOMMENDED READING

Anderson, Neil T. *The Bondage Breaker*. Eugene, OR: Harvest House, 1990.

Backus, William. *Telling Each Other the Truth*. Minneapolis: Bethany House, 1989.

Carnes, Patrick. *Out of the Shadows: Understanding Sexual Addiction*. Center City, MN: Hazelden Foundation, 1992.

Hall, Laurie. *An Affair of the Mind: One Woman's Courageous Battle to Salvage Her Family from the Devastation of Pornography*. Colorado Springs, CO: Focus on the Family, 1996.

Hart, Dr. Archibald D. *Healing Life's Hidden Addictions*. Ann Arbor, MI: Servant Publications, 1990.

Jenkins, Jerry B. *Loving Your Marriage Enough to Protect It*. Chicago: Moody Press, 1993.

Joy, Donald M. *Re-Bonding: Preventing and Restoring Damaged Relationships*. Nappanee, IN: Evangel, 1996.

Wilson, Earl & Sandy, Friesen, Paul & Virginia, Paulson, Larry & Nancy. *Restoring the Fallen: A Team Approach to Caring, Confronting & Reconciling*. Downers Grove, IL: InterVarsity Press, 1997.